Syl'

May y treasure the relationship that you share and may it bring you joy all of your days. Mike & Lisa

LOVE LIFE

LOVE LIFE
HOW TO CREATE A HAPPY RELATIONSHIP AFTER DIVORCE

MIKE DARCEY

This book is dedicated to our children. Until we thought about sharing our stories and knowledge with them, we would have never thought to share this with others and we would have never walked down this path.

Acknowledgements

I am so thankful for my wife, Lisa. She has been my support through the book-writing process and the catalyst for everything this book uncovers.

Table of Contents

Acknowledgments   *vi*
Introduction   *ix*

Chapter One:	This is Your Chance	1
	My Second Chance	6
	Our Second Chance	7
	Your Second Chance	10
Chapter Two:	Build (or Re-build) a Strong Foundation	11
	Residual Hurt	11
	Talk about the Small Stuff	15
	Don't Shy Away from the Big Stuff	16
	Be You (The Best You)	17
	Re-learn Love	20
	Re-define Marriage	21
	Re-define Home	23
Chapter Three:	Avoid the "Unfixables"	25
	Different Core Values	25
	Separate Friends	26
	No Family and Friend Support	27
	Unaligned Goals and Interests	28
	"Opposites Attract"	29
	The SWOT Process	30
Chapter Four:	Diagnose Your Unhealthy Habits	35
	Disagreements	35
	Walking on Eggshells	36
	The Need to be Right	37
	Handle Your Differences	39
	Resolving Conflict	41
	Fight Fair	43
	Prioritize Your Partner's Happiness	46
Chapter Five:	Build Trust	47
	Be Vulnerable	47

	Be Intimate	50
	Let's Talk about Infidelity	51
	Be Communicative	53
Chapter Six:	Connection, Connection, Connection	55
	Time Spent Together and Time Spent Apart	55
	Sharing Space and Comfortable Silence	58
	Create Your Shared Morning Routine	59
	Travel Together	62
Chapter Seven:	Attitude is Truly Everything	64
	Behaving with Courtesy	64
	Have an Attitude of Gratitude	65
	Attitude Check—Meditation	67
Chapter Eight:	Commit Like You Mean It	70
	Commitment	70
	Promote Your Partner	71
	Respect Each Other's Individuality	72
	Plan for the Future	73
Chapter Nine:	LoveLife FAQs	75
	How do I keep my ex from getting under my skin?	76
	How do you talk to your new partner about your past relationship (awkward!)?	77
	How do you introduce your new relationship to your kids from your first marriage?	78
	How do you approach your new spouse's children?	79
	When will this be over?	79
Chapter Ten:	What to Do When the Sh*t Hits the Fan	82
	The Things We've Learned and the Things We Carry	86
	Even Best Laid Plans…	88
	Hitting the Bottom	96
Epilogue:	Don't Stop	99
	About the Author	102

INTRODUCTION

Wow. You opened my book! This is a great sign! Not for me, but for you. It means you are dedicated to taking action and improving your relationship.

Believe me when I tell you that you're taking a big step. I've had my share of painful and destructive relationships and did not care to improve them. It was an easy slide backward, deeper into the pit, unhappy and discontent. I didn't understand how much power I had to create positive change—I didn't even know such change was possible—until I took it upon myself to make it happen. Once I saw how I could build healthy interpersonal habits, my relationships changed for the better. So, whether you are in a happy relationship and your goal is to strengthen it, or you are questioning if your relationship is the right one, the things we have to show you will help.

My wife Lisa and I created the *LoveLife* approach for ourselves. We were both married and divorced before we found each other and knew all too well how painful it is when a marriage falls apart. She and I had learned the sad lesson that you might be grappling with now: love is not enough to create and sustain a happy marriage. It takes work, thoughtfulness, communication, and a plan for when things go off track. We were determined to learn from our failures, dig into our worst habits, and discover the tips and tricks that would keep our relationship at its best.

And our work paid off.

Soon, our friends were marveling at our success and begging us to spill our secrets. It became clear that other couples could apply our methods, so we started LoveLifeCentral.com. Our goal is to help others make their relationships healthier and happier than they dreamed possible.

Before we dive in, there are a few things you should know:

First, you are NOT stuck. You can change yourself and your situation. You can have a thriving relationship—it's not too late. You simply have to begin. That is the key: you must act. Nothing will fix itself.

Take every idea into consideration, not just the advice you need right now. Failure is a blunt teacher, and seeing *our* mistakes may spare you the pain of living them. So while you may reach a section that doesn't apply to your relationship right now, I encourage you not to skip it. I will describe the typical hardships couples face and give strategies you can carry out to break apart issues and emerge on the other side, together and stronger for it.

Keep learning. Gather as many tools as you can hold—the more you have, the better you can tackle any issue that may pop up. The ideas that make up this book are the ones we use most, and we hope they add to (or start) your toolbox for improving your relationship, but don't stop here. Keep reading, learning from others, and trying new ways to make your love life amazing.

Lisa and I want to share our story with the world in the hope that this little contribution can be the catalyst for other couples to want to make their relationship the best they can. We share what we discovered about relationships through research and experience (and, yes, some trial and error) in the chapters to come. We hope that some of these ideas will resonate with you or even inspire you—to overcome a challenge, see your partner in a new and positive light, bring your best to the table, or know that you're worthy of being loved. The unforeseen side effect of writing a book is that, as we examined our lives, we discovered new ways to be the best spouses we can be. We are learning together; it's a win-win!

— Mike Darcey

Chapter One

This is Your Chance

The tale of how Lisa and I came together as a couple is one I've recounted dozens of times. Although our love story is not the focus of this book, a short recap will offer some essential background. (And I love to tell it.)

We met when we were young—we were teenagers—and we most certainly did not have mature feelings or good judgment. We said hello a few times in passing, but we ran in different circles with only one mutual friend. Had someone suggested to us then that Lisa and I might one day marry, I imagine we'd exchange an awkward look: *Him? Her? But we hardly know each other!* Lisa would probably shake her head in disbelief the way it does now when I tell her my latest far-fetched idea. Then we'd brush off the prediction and go our separate ways.

And so our story begins with Lisa and me getting married... to other people.

Like many others in our generation, we both married young, in our early twenties, with little experience and even fewer relationship skills. Lisa and I were living separate lives, yet our marriages took similar paths. We each had grown our families the way people do, with 2.5 kids, nice houses with picket fences out front, stable jobs—the whole bucket—and yet we struggled to make those marriages work. Both Lisa and I excel at taking on responsibility and used that trait to "fix" things in our first marriages. We both (erroneously) believed we could be the hero to rescue our spouses from their shortcomings, but, with time and maturity, we realized our "heroism" had only made us enablers. I could only fix myself. What followed was a clear-eyed (and long-overdue) evaluation of my relationship with my wife, Pamela, and our life together—and our eventual divorce. Lisa's marriage followed a strikingly similar path. We found ourselves heartbroken, exhausted, uprooted, and unsure of what our futures held.

Years passed since high school, and Lisa and I reunited at a mutual friend's wedding. We hit it off immediately. We had plenty to catch up on and shared so many interests. The friendship that never sprouted when we were teenagers found a foothold and some context. It wasn't until several years after that wedding when both of our marriages were headed south and we began to lean on each other for support did it really take root—and it grew fast—but we both were a bit gun-shy. It was impossible to ignore our feelings for each other, but Lisa and I proceeded with caution. Experience is an excellent, blunt, and painful teacher, and we were determined to be "smart" about our budding romance.

Both Lisa and I are analytical and conceptual thinkers, so we chose an almost scientific approach to our love life. From the moment our relationship was official, we strived to create the most loving and supportive partnership we could. We studied the qualities of successful relationships and had lengthy discussions with each other about what we knew was important. Nothing was off limits, as Lisa and I shared our core beliefs, fears, and dreams—even the issues we feared might derail our relationship. We found that as we tackled these difficult (and sometimes scary) topics, our love deepened and we wanted to keep going! It was a cycle: the more we strengthened our relationship, the harder we wanted to work at it! These practices later crystallized into the methods we share with others today.

Here comes the plot twist: My happy marriage with Lisa would have been impossible without my first marriage and divorce. Experience, as I mentioned, is an excellent teacher, and mine has taught me more than I ever would have learned otherwise. That is why I will share my struggle with my first wife, whom we will call Pamela, in the pages to come. Now let me make myself clear: I don't wish to throw my ex-wife under the bus. We were young, naïve, and inexperienced when we got married, and we did the best we could. The failure of our marriage was neither all Pamela's fault nor all mine. The truth is somewhere in between. As you will see, our goal is not to find fault; we want to learn from our experiences.

With that in mind, I'd like to share some of my experiences with you.

Growing up as an only child, I was something of an introvert. I interpreted the world solely through my own lens, never giving much thought to others' perspectives. I held my viewpoint as absolute; my needs, wants, and comforts came first. Needless to say, my default mode was not conducive to dating. Girls, as I found out, wanted to feel as though they mattered, too. Go figure! So it probably won't surprise you to learn that I was not a playboy.

I was the king of first dates, though. My relationships never extended much further than that first dinner or trip to the movies. I was still trying to figure out what I wanted in a girlfriend, and nobody was a match. So I kept looking, kept meeting girls, and kept bailing before a relationship could take hold. Then I met Pamela.

I was a regular at several clubs (or "discotheques," as we called them) in those days, and Pamela was a waitress at the most fun and exciting one in town. She wore this great smile that captivated many men—alluring and friendly but totally unattainable, thanks to her self-imposed rule not to date anyone from the club. There was no shortage of guys who would chase Pamela around the club, testing her commitment to her rule only to find out that she meant business. I was not one of them. In fact, because I was not very outspoken or forward, I stood out from the crowd and caught Pam's eye. We started talking. Then we started dating. I met her young daughter, and we went from there.

Things were pleasant throughout the "getting to know you" phase. I learned Pamela had married before and had a pretty tough life growing up. Her family was big, and they argued often, but it all seemed normal. We had our clashes, sure, but our disagreements seemed minor during that phase. Little did I suspect that these kinds of things were red flags that would resurface again and again. Instead, I charged forward, checking all the relationship-milestone boxes. It wasn't long before marriage seemed like the next reasonable step.

On paper it all made sense. We were at the point in our lives and relationship where we just assumed it was time to get married. What I couldn't see at the time was it wasn't the right relationship. Pam and I were not partners. We didn't have a mutual understanding of what made a marriage. No communication. No shared path. We were like a boat and an airplane latched to each other with a cable; neither one of us could do the things we were meant to do while we bound together.

The distractions of the business, the kids, and day-to-day life kept our marriage survivable. Hard issues went unresolved but unforgotten while smaller, everyday matters barraged the relationship, chipping away at the edges and inching ever closer to our center. When everything was said and done, Pamela and I had been together for twenty-five years and married for twenty. That sounds like a feat—and it was—but the relationship itself was empty, and I had been emotionally vacant from the marriage for some time before we decided to call it quits.

On the spectrum of painful divorces, I'd say ours was right in the middle. Things were not as vicious as you sometimes hear, nor was it friendly, but I committed to making it as painless and easy for Pam as I could. I wanted her to have a good support network, so I dropped my contact with our largest group of friends and let her vilify me to them. I did not petition for joint custody while we were divorcing so she could keep our girls close. I hated myself for giving up my time with my kids, but thought it was the better plan. My business had no equity left, but there was a hefty amount in the house we owned. I gave it all to Pamela so she'd have a nest egg to restart her life again. She understood what I was trying to do, so she agreed to use a single attorney and accepted the divorce process I had laid out. We both sacrificed to make the compromise work.

I still remember looking at Pamela as we stood outside our attorney's office—taking in this woman with whom I'd shared a life, a woman as ready to set off on her separate path as I was—and feeling as though I was truly seeing her. Pamela is a good person with both good and bad qualities. *Human.* Sound familiar? That's all of us. Pam saw the same thing in me. The problem with our relationship was that our qualities put together were neither complementary nor compatible with each other. It was time to start over.

My Second Chance

My divorce marked the lowest point of my life, but it wasn't the only piece going wrong. I also had to shutter my business, the company entrusted to me by my dad. Newly separated, my ego shredded, and with my financial security blown away, I wallowed in despair and self-pity. I only saw my daughters on Sundays, something I never envisioned (and certainly never wanted) for my life. The only lifeline I had was my relationship with Lisa, which at this point had not evolved beyond the just-friends stage; I leaned on her friendship heavily during this period, but there was only so much support she could give.

Then I hit bottom.

It happened on a Sunday, at a party with the kids. I hoped that spending the afternoon with friends and my girls would bring my spirits around, but it didn't. Instead, while the kids were off playing, good ole dad drowned his sorrows in alcohol. When the party came to a close, I was in no condition to be walking, much less to be behind the wheel with my children in the backseat. But I did it anyway. To say I was irresponsible—and an idiot—is an understatement, but that is where I found myself. We were lucky to arrive home in one piece. My daughters understood that Dad had too much; they were frightened, and rightfully so. The kids spent the rest of our time together that weekend watching TV and playing while I slept it off on the couch nearby.

It was later that night—after waking up embarrassed, knowing I had been such a fool—I realized I needed to make a change. *What am I doing?* I wondered. *This is not what my life is meant to be. This is my chance to turn it around.* I realized that I was in the middle of the storm and the tempest, like any other, would someday end. I had terrific kids, and I needed to be an example for them. I had so much to live for, to fight for, and make better. I apologized to my daughters for putting them in that situation and scaring them. I wanted them to be proud of the father I was (and hopefully still am). I had much ground to cover just to get back to square one. My mind churned with ideas on how to get back in the race. My body coursed with energy, ready to take action toward being a better man.

I would be a father worthy of his kids. A friend worthy of forgiveness. I would be a man worthy of an amazing woman's attention. Maybe even her love.

I didn't know a single moment of clarity could do so much until I lived it.

Not everyone gets the opportunity of a second chance? I was lucky, and I knew it. And I was determined to make the most of mine, even if it meant changing my whole life. My entire world. Even if it meant changing *me*.

Our Second Chance

Lisa and I understood that the compatibility and love we shared was unusual right from the get-go. We both agreed our relationship felt as though it was "meant to be," something greater than the sum of its parts. There was a bigger picture we could neither see nor understand, but recognized almost at once. Well, not *at once*. We were too young to see it when we first met, and we didn't see it twenty years later when fate brought us together again. But we understood it thirty years later—the third time's the charm and all that—and determined that we'd give it all we've got.

We made it a point to do things right. There were introductions to family, parents, grandparents, uncles and aunts, and especially the kids. Lisa and I crafted the right moments so we could give these new relationships the best start possible, realizing that things could go off the rails if not handled correctly. Honolulu, despite holding a populous of more than a million people, is still a small town, with two degrees of separation and a gossip grapevine as swift and vicious as kudzu. We realized that we needed to forge each relationship with precision to keep any friction—familial or otherwise—from wreaking havoc on us if we wanted our relationship to last.

It's a funny thing about post-divorce life, but managing your public relations as you get into a new relationship is crucial. (Inevitably there are those who have your ex's interests in mind and may broadcast their judgment and perceived wrongdoing against you.) It is much better to do some "marketing" to position your relationship in the best light so you can move forward with your life, unhampered by your past.

It worked for Lisa and me. As our relationship grew stronger, so did our circle of influence with other people, and even the grapevine would tell stories of how happy she and I were together. We were doing something different, something that set our relationship apart, and our friends took notice. It wasn't long before they started asking for advice. Slowly, I realized that my "second chance" was developing into something much bigger than I ever anticipated. I had been evolving into a different person. The introverted (okay, let's call them what they were: self-centered) habits I'd maintained throughout my life had given way to a new external focus.

First, I learned how to be a better friend, co-worker, and family member. I made it a point to enhance the meaningfulness of my existing close relationships with friends. I became more involved with my high school classmates and enjoyed getting to know those guys at a different level than we could have ever reached in high school. I spend more time getting to know my work acquaintances and figuring out how to provide them some value. I joined a personal development community, Best Year Ever Blueprint, and its exclusive mastermind group, Quantum Leap Mastermind. In the last ten years, I've also met my biological father (whom I fondly call "Bio-Dad") and his family. The clan is large and woven into the fabric of the Hawaiian Islands. I have maintained our connection and want to get to know them better while maintaining and enhancing the relationships with my existing family. Improving the relationships around me is the part of my transformation I consider the most rewarding.

I also learned to be a better partner. My second chance with Lisa is the best thing that ever happened to me, and I tell anyone willing to listen how wonderful my relationship with her is and how lucky I am. I want to evolve into the best person I can be for her. I want her to adore me and keep me by her side forever. She makes me want to work hard at being a good man. We feel our relationship is bigger than the both of us.

Your Second Chance

Do you believe that you can undergo the same evolution? It starts with the choice to make yourself better. What kind of friend, parent, sibling, co-worker, boss, partner, or spouse do you want to be?

You have that chance right now. Your second (or third or fourth or hundredth) chance. What will you do with it?

Chapter Two

Build (or Re-build) a Strong Foundation

You wouldn't construct a house without laying a sturdy foundation, right? Foundations are important in every aspect of life. The foundation of your relationship needs to be the strong point you come back to when everything gets shaky. But first, you need to clear the way for those cornerstones—and that means taking a good hard look at the lingering pain points that might be taking up space in your life and your psyche. Then you'll be ready to build.

Residual Hurt

Dealing with the residual hurt from a previous relationship is hard. Let's face it, every relationship that has ended (whether friend, lover, work associate, church, etc.) did so because it did not serve at least one end of the partnership and someone got hurt. But that doesn't mean the experience cannot serve you now. Can you change your perception and see it as a valuable piece of learning? Can you look at the worst moments of your life, whether you screwed up or were screwed over, and see them as an opportunity for improvement?

Turning your "baggage" into knowledge is an essential step toward a fruitful new relationship.

There is no better learning process than to try and fail and then try something else—much akin to the process of elimination. How better to discern what you want? What surer way to discover your deal-breakers? Unfortunately, many people don't figure out their values, desires, and dislikes before they walk down the aisle. That is why half of all marriages fail.

I was among them. I did not understand what I wanted in a loving relationship and had no clue what my deal-breakers were. When I got into my first marriage, I had a sincere (and naïve) commitment to something I barely understood. My lack of self-education ensured that I could not love Pamela the way she wanted. I felt like I had settled for "good enough" because tying the knot was what all reasonable people my age were doing—and I was determined to stick it out to the end. Eventually, however, I had so much hurt and resentment built up against Pamela that the relationship ended, predictably, with pain on both sides.

I have found that time and reflection heal wounds, even those that were self-inflicted. Also, taking the time to figure out what was great and bad with Pamela gave me guidance on how I wanted to focus the direction of my new relationship with Lisa. Hurt gave way to learning, and the pain subsided. Pamela and I, although not best friends, are still friendly and have moved on with our lives. We have our kids in common, and parenthood keeps us in touch with care and concern for one another.

How can you learn from and then clear away your residual hurt?

Look at your past relationships and analyze what worked (and what blew up in your face) to come up with your list of desires and deal-breakers. Many of us, myself included, bury our past pains and scars as best we can—and as quickly as we can. Perhaps masking it over is a defense mechanism needed to get us through hard times, but it is helpful to look back and discover the educational pieces. As Winston Churchill said, "Those that fail to learn from history are doomed to repeat it."

If you look back to learn, you will identify strengths about yourself that you did not know you had. You may also find your weaknesses. Both are important, and knowing them will help your future relationships. However, sometimes situations are unpredictable, and all your preparation is not enough. The relationships you thought were solid fell apart while others sprang up. Perhaps someone unexpected stepped up and helped you through the mess. Maybe they were there temporarily, never to be seen again; perhaps they became part of your new life structure.

One thing is sure: shit happens and life changes in ways you cannot expect, but you can still have contingency plans in place. You should do your darnedest to prepare for potential eventualities as best you can; just know there will be things you do not and cannot expect.

For me, all of this is true; I couldn't have expected my divorce with Pamela or the close of my business—and I would never have fathomed the two might end at the same time. Sure, those rough experiences sparked a time of great learning and change in me, but, before my personal renaissance, I was in pretty bad shape from years of not learning from my failures. Thus, I was not in a healthy place; I did not reflect on how to compensate for my weaknesses or how to capitalize on my strengths, and I had gobs of resentment building up that I thought would just go away if I ignored it.

Although I now take responsibility for both the divorce and the business collapse, that was not always the case. I needed to step back from the situation after a long time had passed to look at things with a somewhat objective eye. My arrogant decision-making could have been the root of the company closing, and my fundamental lack of understanding of relationships was undoubtedly partly responsible for my divorce. After looking at those situations through a new lens, I can see my faults, and I have learned from them.

- I've learned more about trust, and who deserves mine and who does not.

- I learned the hard way that life can toss your best-laid plans overboard.

- I learned that I have the internal fortitude to survive the world crashing down around me and now know, without a shadow of a doubt, that I could do it again if I had to.

- I understand that living a life with a purpose is the ONLY way to live, and I have found mine—this book is a testament to the passion I have for Lisa and my relationship with her.

Everyone has a different life. I am telling you my story, but yours is just as worthy and more compelling to you. Once time has gotten you over the hump, I urge you to look back at your pain and find your own gems to learn from, make adjustments to, and grow from in the end. I was astonished at what I found when I studied the time my life was falling apart. There was so much to learn! Some changes were temporary, while others I made permanent. The big changes came from the lessons I learned from the lowest point of my life.

For example, I learned to speak up.

Talk about the Small Stuff

What's for dinner? It's such a small thing, isn't it? But it was a question I was genuinely afraid to ask Lisa. The question was a bona fide landmine in my first marriage and I had a lot of residual hurt around it.

Pamela and I didn't cook much; time was often short and eating dinner out was a regular occurrence. Sometimes we cooked, but even then, the process of picking a meal was painful. Pamela was not usually a decision maker and relinquished the dinner duties to me—but just because she didn't want to pick, it didn't mean she didn't have an opinion. And that made "What's for Dinner" a hostile guessing game, in which I feebly tried to suss out what Pam felt like eating... or it became a painful game of elimination on where we would NOT eat. Best-case scenario, I could narrow the field down to thirty choices, leaving me to guess what might make her happy. If I answered wrong, it would be a fight.

My fear of asking where we might eat lingered long after the end of the marriage. Lisa and I had to deal with that—and, admittedly, she was confused why something so innocuous as where to go for date night was paralyzing for me. So we identified the problem and talked through simple solutions, starting with "Mike answers first." I am pretty much omnivorous and will eat anything, but if I have a craving, I say so right out the gate. Ninety percent of the time, Lisa says, "Good choice!" Now and then, she'll voice a different craving (which I happily accommodate). Over time, my residual pain over finding a place to eat or what to eat has diminished entirely.

Don't Shy Away from the Big Stuff

Picking dinner options is a simple issue, but what about the important stuff? What about being afraid to talk about an unhappy situation because you don't want it to blow up into a fight? Well, guess what? You should do it anyway. It's better to speak up and have the battle right away than to let it fester. It's never too early (or too late) to establish your lines of communication. When there's an issue, talk about it! Residual hurt remains and multiplies until you identify it and address it.

You are what you do. Everything you do defines who you are. Your behavior in public, what you do when no one is looking, your biases—they all make you who you are. And they ripple out. So do you want everyone you encounter to get hit by the consequences of your residual hurt? Your friends and family become unintentional targets of this negative energy. Potentially the most harm is done to your kids (if you have them). Like Lisa tells me, the fruit doesn't fall far from the tree. Be aware of ways you could be accidentally hurting those around you out of your residual hurt.

Now that you have had the chance to inspect your residual hurt, we need to put the foundations together to build a successful root to your relationship. It's time to set the cornerstones, starting with... *you*.

Be You (The Best You)

Who do you want to be? Who are you when you're at your best? How does your "best you" fill your life? Write out your priorities, no matter how big or small.

For each item you've listed, ask yourself: "Am I living out this value?" "Do I put my relationships first?" and so on. Ask those who know you best to chime in, too. Ask them if you are genuinely taking on these characteristics. You may not be the person you think you are, but that should not stop you from becoming that person! It will be hard work, but I know you have it in you. You already have all the reasons in the world to become the person you want to be; all you need is a little nudging to get it done. There is no excuse not to try to be better than you are now.

Over my lifetime, I've tried to be an excellent athlete, one of the cool kids, a successful businessman, a world-class singer—the list goes on and on. What I found every time was that there was always someone who did those things better than I could. No matter what level of success I reached in those areas, there was always someone who could outperform me, and so I would move on to the next mark and strive to attain that. I made it a point not to be content with that area of life until I achieved the new goal.

Then came the crash. Out of the ashes, I realized that everyone has a story I know nothing about. Everyone has a struggle I don't understand. Everyone is on a different path in life than I am. I am not competing against everyone else; *I am in competition with my former self.* I needed to set happiness destinations that were my own, not anyone else's.

Recently I happened upon a TEDx talk called, "The Art of Being Yourself," which I highly recommend to everyone. In her speech, Caroline McHugh, the founder and CEO of IDOLOGY, says that the primary goal of your life is to be the best and most authentic you that you can be. She poses three questions during her talk that are a good starting point for anyone:

"Who do you think you are?"
"What do you expect from life?"
"What does life expect from you?"

These are not questions you ask once and move on. Think of them as a doctor's check-up or a financial statement and use them to periodically check in with yourself and monitor your progress. I set my personal goals of health, wealth, friends, and happiness. As long as I am making progress, I am happy. Will I ever reach the pinnacle of any of those aims? Maybe. Maybe not. But I will be satisfied with the headway I have made.

What makes me incredibly me is everything about me is all me. The history of my childhood, the not fitting in during my teenage years, the working every spot in my family company, the collapse of that same company, the failed marriage, and the returning on the other side with a renewed purpose, a new fabulous relationship that is primary in my life and everything else comes second—I am all those things, and all those experiences, and all those lessons. There is no other life I would want more than my own.

But this chapter isn't just about you. It is also about your partner. I encourage you to use Caroline McHugh's questions to check in with your relationship, too:

"Who do we think we are as a couple?"

"What do we expect from our life together?"

"What does life expect from us?"

And I'd add one more:

"How can we be our best selves together?"

This question was a powerful one for Lisa and me, and it led to a whole new (and purpose-giving) mindset for us. We wanted to set an example for our kids, to demonstrate a loving and supportive marriage and teach them to expect no less for themselves. This purpose infused our choices as we live those manifestations out in the open. Since the start of our relationship, Lisa and I knew it was something that was much bigger than the two of us. It was something we needed to share with the world, not as a boasting point but as a light for others. That has been the underlying purpose in our relationship and the reason for this book.

Everything we do feeds our primary purpose. We pursue activities, work, and even friendships that encourage our relationship and cut out the things that undermine it. Look at all aspects of your life through the lens of your shared purpose and decide if it stays or if it goes. It may be tough as first, but once you get started, looking at things through that lens gets easier and easier. Our shared sense of purpose—to be a light for other couples—influences our choices every day.

None of us are perfect, so expect times of weakness and failure. Just make sure you get back up and put yourself back on your path. Be the very best "you" you can. Then be the very best "us."

Re-learn Love

What is love? It is different things to different people, but re-learning what love really means to *you* is another essential cornerstone of your foundation. There are so many opinions about love that we could go on for years trying to break things down further. So let's get a little clarity from the ancient Greeks, who broke love down into seven different facets:

Eros is the romantic love between new lovers. Often it is characterized by physical signs of affection and sexual attraction. It is intense but rarely lasts as long as the other types of love, and often depends on the behavior or personality of one partner.

Philia is the kind of love between platonic friends or friendship between close friends. It is usually based on mutual respect and is not characterized as intense. It is easy to accept one another, as differences are less essential to the survival of the love in this relationship.

Storge is the love between a parent and a child. I think of it as unconditional and not limited to a parent and child. Love and acceptance are almost always given.

Agape is the love of mankind or the world at large. It is the love of their fellow man regardless of how well you know each other. Charity and volunteerism characterize Agape love. The people who volunteer and do things for other people who cannot do anything to pay them back are practicing this kind of love.

Ludus is a playful, flirty, casual, fun love. It's a shallow connection and may even include multiple people. There is often deception and a disregard for the other person's emotions.

Pragma is practical love or obligation. Love based on common sense and reason. It is the love that long-term married relationships often become.

Philautia is the love of one's self. There is high confidence in one's self-worth and with that a high disregard for others.

Over the course of a relationship, you will likely experience several of these different types of love. *Eros* starts out as *Ludus* where flirting and fun turns into a love relationship. The hope is that *Eros* turns into *Pragma* that can stand the test of time—that's what we are here to help you do—and a fundamental knowledge of simple definitions like these will help you navigate your feelings as they change (hopefully) for the better.

On top of definitions, there are many ways to express love. Gary Chapman did an excellent job in describing how we give and receive love in *The Five Love Languages*. He has characterized them as behaviors we do to show our love: physical touch, acts of service, giving and receiving of gifts, quality time, and words of affirmation. It's important to identify which two or three languages you and your partner prefer to use to give love and which languages you prefer to receive. The possibility that these don't match between you and your partner is less important than recognizing the language your partner wants to receive love in so you can provide them with it, and vice versa. We suggest that you read Mr. Chapman's books for a detailed examination of the Love Languages.

Re-define Marriage

Marriage, as well as love, also needs to be redefined for a healthy foundation. Many perspectives on marriage are legitimate, but for the sake of trying to create the best possible relationship, marriage needs to be redefined to match your target.

Marriage is a commitment to stay together, come what may. You vow to stay with the other person until death breaks that promise for you. Clearly, with a divorce rate higher than fifty percent for first marriages (and worse than that for subsequent marriages), most people are not taking that promise seriously.

Starting with that commitment, and wanting to create the best relationship possible, the definition of marriage should include other themes as well.

There needs to be an effort by you and your partner to create joy and laughter. Everyone wants fun in their lives. That is a desire that can bring two people closer together. It's an easy one, so you want to build that in your relationship. Having your marriage be a place where you can feel safe laughing at yourself with your partner is a great goal. If you are a person who cannot cope with your loved one laughing at some small silly mishap, you will need to realize that it is OK. Start small. You may try to adopt a perspective of bringing a very healthy joy and laughter to your partner and the relationship. Learn to laugh at yourself. If your partner has difficulty with this, be gentle. Perhaps by showing that you can laugh at yourself, you will also encourage your partner to do the same.

Traditionally, marriage is set up like a job. Even the ceremony tells you the things you will do and not do, like a job description: love them, take care of them when they are sick, feed them, house them. Here is where we all need to redefine what marriage means to us. I implore you to consider the following shift in perspective. Your marriage is an adventure above and beyond any other earthly relationship that you will nurture, protect, and enjoy. It's up to you to define what that means to you.

Re-Define Home

Home is a place where you and your family are most comfortable, but I challenge you to shift your mindset here, too. Many have said home is where the heart is. I would extend that to say home is wherever the relationship between you and your partner is strongest. In our case, home is an embrace between Lisa and me. It does not matter whether we are in our house, a restaurant, or at the beach. When we are together, we are home, and the most persuasive evidence to us is our hugs.

If you moved to another state, or another country, or another planet, as long as you were together, you would not lose your home. If your house burned to the ground or got destroyed by a hurricane, you would not lose your home. As long as you are together, you will always have the comfort of home and the knowledge that all the rest of everything is just stuff. And all that stuff matters much less than your relationship.

Because home is now your relationship, a fundamental theme is that there has to be harmony. You need to be a place of mental and physical safety for each other. Ideally, your home will be a place you can't wait to get to and dread leaving. This environment between the two of you is where building and taking care of trust starts. How can you bring more harmony into your home?

Home is also where stability lives. Like building trust, both partners need to provide security to each other. Part of the commitment to make your best life together is to stick to your word. Say what you will do and do what you say. There are always issues that will arise that might be (or are already) sensitive or volatile. You should approach the subject of how to deal with sensitive issues when the relationship is harmonious so you can create strategies and a framework to accommodate these kinds of sensitive topics when there is stress on the relationship. For example when a conversation that will inconvenience one partner comes up (say, for instance, having your mother-in-law come to live with you), having a process in place to discuss the issue rationally is key to building stability and trust.

Purposeful love, a committed marriage, a harmonious home, and your best YOU—those are the four cornerstones of a solid foundation. As a final note for this chapter, I will encourage you to lay that foundation on common ground, a place where you and your partner see things from the same or similar perspectives. Explore your angles on some simple issues to find where you agree and why. Build on those items and find as many points of agreement as you can. Having a base of shared values will make tackling a sensitive subject more comfortable because you know you have more in common than in contention. All these together will make your relationship so strong that it can withstand any storm.

Building your *LoveLife* foundation is something you can do at any stage of your relationship. In fact, you don't need to be in a relationship at all! Doing the work of clearing out your residual pain and laying your cornerstones happens at the individual level first, then it can be shared. And, as we're about to see, you want to make sure you're sharing your foundation with the right person.

Chapter Three

Avoid the "Unfixables"

You can change many things about yourself, but you can't change someone else. That's why it's so important to steer clear of "unfixables" and stay true to your foundation—even if that means NOT dating someone you like. For example, if your dream in life is to have a big family, do not get into a relationship with someone who does not want children. Sometimes their feelings may evolve, but you will never change them by force. Try, and you'll only build resentment and anger.

This chapter is about the red flags you should never ignore.

Different Core Values

Having different core values come into play can be tough on a relationship. If your moral scale differs significantly from your partner's, you can and likely will have a handful of issues to deal with when one partner becomes frustrated with the lack of agreement. Consider honesty or faithfulness, for example. If those two virtues mean different things to each partner, that's a real hindrance to creating the best relationship possible.

Pamela and I had vast differences in our core values—some were direct opposites of each other—and that is a hard thing to change. For example, she valued certainty, stability, consistency, dependability, and connection to other people, while I liked surprises, pushing the edge, trying new things, creativity, and doing things on my own. She didn't like to take risks, but I did. We also had shared values like generosity, balance, and assertiveness, but where we differed made us operate in divergent ways, and that made working together (crucial for any marriage) very difficult.

Lisa and I share our core values. We share love, gratitude, selflessness, flexibility, and harmony, which makes how we operate with each other pretty smooth. With similar core values, life together is easier from the start.

Separate Friends

Who do you spend most of your time with? If you spend more time with your friends than you do with your partner, that's a red flag. It often promotes time spent apart and varied interests, which can be the wedge between two people. Having your own groups of friends is not necessarily a bad thing, but a significant amount of time spent apart makes it harder to build a better relationship.

Pamela and I had different friends, and we had friends we shared. In the beginning, we were both terrific about blending into our diverse circle of friends. Over time, though, I noticed that Pamela didn't care for some of my best buddies. She would beg out of coming to a dinner or party if certain people were in attendance.

That left me in a no-win situation: I could go without her, for which she'd feel resentful, or I could stay home and feel resentful toward her for making me stay home. Other times we would plan to go, but a fight would erupt an hour before we were to leave and cause us both stay home.

It's one thing if these fights happened once or twice, but after a dozen times, it had become a clear pattern. As time passed, even though I tried to fight it, that wedge drove itself further and further into the wound, and our different sets of friends became a huge obstacle in our marriage.

Lisa and I, perhaps because we are so alike, are easily drawn into and well liked by each other's friend groups. We feel like there is no such thing as "Mike's friends" or "Lisa's friends"; they are *our* friends. It is a wonderful feeling that draws us closer together rather than driving us apart.

No Family and Friend Support

More often than not, your family and close friends know you more objectively than you know yourself. And that means they are more apt to notice when something is off. When your new relationship doesn't have the support of your family and close friends, it may indicate that they see something you're missing. So, presuming they have your best interests at heart, pay attention when your friends dislike or distrust your partner.

The relationship between Pamela and my mother was a prime example of what I'm talking about here. They flat-out didn't like each other and all the passive-aggressive behaviors were making things so bad that it was easier just to avoid any interaction between them than to enjoy family time together. Once again, my arrogance thought it would be fine for all of us to work in the family business together, which only put them in the same space eight hours a day, five days a week. This was not a delight either. What was I thinking??? I should have seen the signs.

With Lisa and I, our relationships with our in-laws and each other's families are all we could hope they would be. There is a lot of love shared in the households and getting together is something we enjoy as often as we can.

Unaligned Goals and Interests

I am going out on a limb with this one, as I don't believe varied goals and interests are sure sign of a problem, BUT I do think it's worthy of your attention. Having goals and interests is a beautiful thing, and everyone should have them. I do think they should be discussed at length to see what your goals and interests are and to see how they may bring you together or perhaps pull you apart as a couple. Lisa and I discuss ours regularly as, over time, goals and interests adjust. Usually, a discussion about a goal or interest will illuminate what one person wants to develop in their lives and how the relationship fits into their plans. Just be sure that your goals and interests don't take away from your partner's.

"Opposites Attract"

Being in a close relationship with someone can be hard enough without adding significant character differences. When personalities are too dissimilar, at least one partner will likely compromise some facet of his or her identity or feel as though they are not living up to some standard set by the other person.

When people have differing personalities, they tend to display symptoms of unhealthy relationships. Often these couples spend more time apart with friends, and have different interests, different core values, and different goals. Relationships have survived in this manner, but this is not the ideal, close relationship that you want for the long term.

My case is an excellent example of how a relationship didn't work because of the "opposites attract" myth. I blend into the crowd and feel comfortable in the middle somewhere. Being on a stage the center of attention was never something I felt comfortable doing and never felt warranted that I belonged there, anyway. But I liked girls who had some notoriety, who stood out in a crowd, and had stunning good looks (well, who didn't when they were in high school?). I believed the smaller someone's physical stature, the larger their personality, and I liked a large personality, so I was also attracted to petite women. Pamela fit all these descriptions.

Those relationships never worked out, for several reasons. Those types of women, if they had an initial interest, got bored with my quiet, homely life and needed quite a different level of excitement and energy. In my mind, those women were shooting for the stars, while I was content plugging along in my life. We would spend time with our respective sets of friends and had different directions in life.

Even in my first marriage, by the time I was interested in making the marriage work, there were so many obstacles in the road to try to fix after those bumps had turned into mountains and new barriers continued to pop up in front of us.

The thing to keep in mind is that these red flags are not the same as "unfixables," at least, not in every case. With some attentiveness and proactive action, you can learn what those red flags have to teach you and keep them from ruining your relationship. And I've got the perfect exercise for checking in with your partner: SWOT.

The SWOT Process

Now that we have identified some things that may likely be difficult to navigate through, the question is, how do you find these problems and determine whether they are deal-breakers? Well, the approach we used to evaluate our relationship is very much like a strategic planning session that businesses implement when a significant improvement is needed in the company. A SWOT evaluation is used to identify the *Strengths, Weaknesses, Opportunities,* and *Threats,* but instead of discussing a business, we'll look at those things in the marriage.

If a deal-breaker cannot be fixed, it's time to make a decision. The inevitable result of maintaining a relationship with an unfixable deal-breaker is, at best, a life of mediocrity.

The SWOT process gives the chance to evaluate costs and benefits. SWOT stands for strengths, weaknesses, opportunities, and threats. In business, we look at this kind of metric regularly to determine our place in the market and how to improve our standing, efficiency, income, and future outlook. It can be done as simply or as elaborately as you want. In relationships between two people, it's really about them writing things down on four lists, one for each heading. Strengths and weaknesses are internal to the relationship (or company). Opportunities and threats are external. Strengths and opportunities are good things that you try to capitalize and use to your advantage, while weaknesses and threats are things you need to defend. Use this knowledge to take advantage of every opportunity in the relationship, identifying the items that naturally lend themselves to easy implementation toward creating and maintaining the best possible relationship!

Let's start with "**S**." A strength you could capitalize on in your relationship is that you have love and care for each other, and you wouldn't want to bring harm to the other person. Or, maybe you have marketable skills with a good long-term future outlook so that financial matters should not be a problem for a long time. Strengths are something you or your partner brings to the relationship that adds to its value.

One of the significant advantages Lisa and I have is the ability to discuss anything and everything. We have enough trust in the relationship to know that our conversation is valid, honest, and strictly between us. The question you are trying to answer is: *what do you do well as a couple, and what are your experiences or skills that add to your relationship to make that possible?* Next, recognize those strengths and put effort into using them as much as you can, trying to get momentum going for the positive future of the relationship.

On to the "**W**." A weakness could be that you dislike your in-laws, or you have a medical condition that could shorten your life.

It could be a weakness in the relationship itself, like the many in my relationship with Pamela. It could be that one partner cannot have children. Sometimes you can change a weakness and sometimes you cannot. The questions here are: *what are the things we do as a couple that shakes our relationship's foundation, what do we not know how to do, and what things are lacking in our relationship?* These each need to be examined to see whether they will cause long-term problems, and thus become deal-breakers.

Next is the "**O**." There are always opportunities, especially for relationships. Opportunities to improve a relationship could be as simple as a conversation with the right person or finding a good book to help change your perspective on the relationship. It could be a trip around the world to have a wonderful time together. It is something from the outside that could improve your position or condition of your relationship. The question here is: *what is out there that can help us improve our relationship?* Latch on to these things! Leverage them to strengthen your relationship and iron out weaknesses or threats.

Last, the "**T**." Threats are prolific. There are all kinds of threats to strong relationships, and they are often hidden. Hear this: things are not always so obvious. A friendly relationship that one person has that drives a wedge between you and your partner, a new hobby that takes time away from the only time you and your partner can spend together, a financial downturn, a serious illness, these are all threats that can affect your relationship. Some of them are non-existent or far off in the distance; some of them are just outside your front door. Ask: *What are any threats, possibly hidden from view, that can damage your relationship?*

Analyze those threats to see if there is imminent danger there or something that is best to nip in the bud. Address the threats first, and then the associated weaknesses that go with those threats. What Lisa and I do is pair up the tools we have discovered through our strengths and opportunities with the weaknesses and put them to work on that threat. Over time, each threat will be met with a tool that changes or addresses a particular vulnerability. And, if you can't find the right tool, use your opportunities to find one!

If we can get to that point of awareness of our relationship, we hope to be what Stephen Covey described as sharpening the saw. We will run the process as often as necessary, at regular intervals, to keep improving the relationship.

Logistically, the SWOT session breaks into brainstorming, prioritization, solutions, and execution plans. The brainstorming part of the meeting is just throwing out any and all items that fall into the four categories. This requires looking at real things that are already in play as well as potential issues that could be a possibility. No answers are evaluated; they are only listed. The more ideas put on paper, the more accessible the remaining sections will be.

The prioritization part of the session is where you look at everything in any category to decide if they are real or perceived, then, for the weaknesses and threats, determine which of these is the most imminent and might become a real obstacle to your relationship.

The solutions phase of the journey is just that, trying to figure out the best ways to overcome the top few weaknesses and prevent the prioritized threats. Your job is to figure out what strategy would diminish the weaknesses and threats, or at least keep them at bay. This is the section that will be most difficult, as there are many ways to skin a cat. Pick the answers you both feel comfortable with implementing. Here is where you start to be a team and work on the same issues from the same side with the same end goal: improvement of the relationship you share.

The execution phase is where you take the solutions you now have agreed upon and put them into place to better the relationship. Then comes the feedback process. Test a solution, then provide feedback. Is it working the way you expected? Do you need to make any adjustments? Continue to check in from time to time and re-execute until the weakness has been overcome, or the threat has completely gone away.

Hopefully, the SWOT process will allow you to look carefully at the things that could be potential unfixables in your relationship and give you space to grow and problem-solve to overcome them.

Chapter Four

Diagnose Your Unhealthy Habits

You don't need to become an expert to diagnose the unhealthy habits affecting your relationship. These are your weaknesses in your relationship that, like cancer, will grow and metastasize, eventually killing the connection between you and your partner.

Disagreements

Disagreeing on issues happens regardless of the harmony in your relationship. The frequency and intensity of those disagreements is the real issue. Without the ability to "agree to disagree," discussion can quickly turn into an argument, allowing resentment and bitterness to fester. Many times, these nasties will show up as passive-aggressive behavior or uncalled-for unpleasantness. As the downfall progresses, arguing in the relationship becomes the norm, until there are more disagreements than agreements.

In my relationship with Pamela, one of our usual arguments was our lack of communication. It was one thing she would always point out; she was communicative, and I was not. In my mind, I could not communicate my thoughts and feelings to Pamela because it was far easier to keep harmony in the household by not saying much at all. This silence was a huge communication problem, and we had no strategy to get past it, no path to resolution.

Now in my relationship with Lisa, when we have disagreements, I welcome the conversation whether or not it presents a potential fight. In fact, my attitude has changed so much that once there is anything that is even a small issue, I push myself into meeting it head on. We confront it before it has the chance to grow or to spread to other areas of our life. We actively and creatively tackle these little issues, making sure we each know the relationship between us is more important than any of these small issues.

Walking on Eggshells

It's a HUGE red flag if you feel like you need to tiptoe around most conversations. This feeling of walking on eggshells is a sure-fire sign that hidden issues need attention. Another symptom of this is the feeling that every action needs to be calculated to avoid conflict. You feel as though you have to be on guard, all the time, ready to put up an emotional barricade on a moment's notice. These are indicators that you may have differences in core values or a significant lack of trust, often causing fights that nobody wants, but no one is willing to back down, either. No one should tolerate those kinds of situations. There should be absolutely no fear of speaking up in a healthy relationship.

At the start of my relationship with my first wife, eggshells were non-existent. There was a time when both of us could say whatever we wanted and it was fine. Slowly, specific hot buttons emerged. Not all at once, but more like a cavity, where a little pain would start, and then it would worsen. Hot topics kept popping up until there was little we could safely talk about—everything else was a potential root canal.

I wanted so badly to avoid conflict that I gave myself over to the eggshell mindset. Any time my interaction with Pamela became uncomfortable, I tried to dodge it to spare myself the ensuing fight. This behavior fits well with my non-confrontational, non-explosive personality, but it also prolonged and inflamed the more profound issues we had. With Lisa, I learned to overcome my natural inclinations and confront problems in a healthy, non-inflammatory way. It may help you to learn to confront problems as I did, but the right remedy for you will depend on you and your situation. In all cases, however, the feeling that you need to walk on eggshells around another person is a sign that something is off.

The Need to be Right

Both Lisa and I experienced partners that needed to have the last word of any argument.

Interestingly, we handled it in similar ways. While our partners needed to be right, Lisa and I both had the desire to have peace and harmony in the house. Even when we knew our opinions were valid, we would concede to our partners for the sake of an early end to the argument. We all got what we wanted: we got peace in the house, and our partners got a win.

What we didn't realize is the long-term effect of such a strategy. The more we conceded things, the more our partners would push for things to be right about, and the more we would admit, and so on. Lisa and I separately felt resentment build up, holding it inside for the sake of peace. What each of us failed to understand is that the power and respect within the relationship slowly crept toward our partner's side until there was none left for us.

A closer look at the root of the issue is warranted. What happened in my previous marriage, in my opinion, was Pamela replaced value with power. When our communication had deteriorated, there was probably a point where she questioned the value she had in the relationship, a worthwhile question when you feel isolated from your partner. She couldn't ask because such a volatile subject undoubtedly would cause an argument and so was to be avoided at all costs. A diminishing value in a relationship usually goes along with a diminishing level of self-esteem. This, too, was surely something Pam felt, as I did not affirm her because of our communication issues. Additionally, where the relationship was going was very uncertain—a scary thing! Arguing and being right gives a sense of power and control and, with it, a sense of certainty. My guess is that to feel she had value in the relationship, something tangible to grasp, she would secure the power of being right. This gave her a position of power she mistook for being valuable to the relationship.

Unfortunately, that desire for power is addictive, a habit that is hard to break. It also builds up resentment and defensiveness—the steel wedge that turns a tiny crack into a gaping chasm with only a few bad interactions.

What is the solution?

There is no one right answer. Look for bits of truth in your partner's perspective and try to evaluate why you might feel resistance to their view. *Is it a deep-rooted belief preventing me from seeing things the same way? Is it some past hurt that complicates my understanding of the issue? Could it be a belief or a pain that my partner has that keeps them from seeing my perspective on this issue?* These questions will help combat each person's need to be right. In our case, we try to continue the conversation about the issue until we find a mutual understanding.

Accepting the other person's point of view soothes many ills, even if you cannot come to a consensus. When you get to that point, ask each other, "Is the issue worth damaging the relationship for?" The answer for us is always that our relationship is much more important than that issue. We seek to be open to the other person's point of view rather than reactive to their stance on a topic. We try to evaluate our interactions during our disagreements based not on who is right or wrong but on who is kinder and more compassionate.

Handle Your Differences

We've already discussed the "opposites attract" myth, but there will always be differences between you and your partner. In my relationship with Pamela, the differences were evident. Over time these individual differences grew, like blades of grass in the cracks of a sidewalk, and broke the relationship apart. Differences we ignored wedged into the small cracks in our relationship, eventually shattering the marriage—death by a thousand little cuts.

Lisa and I have many similarities, but we still have our fair share of differences, as with every relationship will. Let's take a closer look at one. Lisa and I drive very differently. Let's just say she is the cautious one. Although, we have very different styles of driving, we have never gotten into an argument about how each other drives. One, because it is deeply ingrained in our minds that the way we drive is the right way, and second, defending our way of driving is not more important than our relationship. However, I have noticed that, over time, my driving has changed when Lisa is in the car with me. As long as we are together, it is time well spent. I find that I drive slower, I give the car ahead of me more space, I signal more, and I am way more courteous to other drivers than I would be otherwise. I know this makes her feel safe, and her comfort is important to me. We live by the rule: "Don't sweat the small stuff, and it's all small stuff." Something that would be a huge deal becomes a minor bump and a learning opportunity.

Here is another example of our differences and how we handled it. Just a week ago, Lisa and I were at the store to find a food processor and a few things we needed around the house. Lisa is cognizant of the storage space of our house and so wanted something simple. I like a lot of horsepower in my kitchen appliances. Much to my surprise, the store only had two food processors: one sleek and simple, and one with horsepower galore and every blade and container combination available. I did my sales pitch for the bigger-better-faster one, and, with not so much as a thought, Lisa asked, "Does this smaller one do ninety percent of the food processing we need?" Without saying another word, I put the little one in the shopping cart. I trusted her judgment and deferred to her. I had to remember the silly food processor was not worth putting a wedge in between us, no matter how small.

Resolving Conflict

In my previous marriage, I did not spend time thinking about my actions in the conflict. I would argue minor issues and continue the argument until I won, or, if I never gained the victory, it would be a bone of contention for a lifetime. At the time, it was worth the fight over the value of the relationship. Some items would always be an issue; one of us never allowed it to be resolved. There was a point when I wouldn't respond at all if an issue arose. Looking back at those interactions now, what appeared to be a communication issue was made much larger because of how I handled it. What I did not recognize was that those items would would drive us apart further and further until we were worlds apart, with nothing to draw us back together. I am not proud of how I handled things in those years, but I'm willing to talk about it if it helps you to recognize your patterns.

Since that time, I have come to recognize this shortcoming in myself and have committed to fixing this flaw in my personality. One of the critical things Lisa and I have put in place to aid conflict resolution is we pick our battles. Some differences don't matter at all. Do you like ketchup on your hotdog or do you like mustard? No one cares; it's not worth fighting over.

There is a myriad of other topics that are worth discussing but may not be worth fighting over. A good filter for evaluating a topic is to look at the totality of the issue in perspective of the value of the relationship itself. If fighting about the issue is worth damaging the relationship, then go ahead and fight about it. If it's not worth hurting the relationship, bring it up as a discussion, but drop it before it becomes a fight; it's just not worth it. Fighting can get out of hand quickly when emotions don't get dealt with in a controlled manner. When the issue is not worth losing the relationship over, learn to agree to disagree; then stop fighting (hopefully you didn't even start!!). Both partners in the relationship need to internalize this approach, or it won't work. This is the best way to get through an issue with multiple right answers.

Most issues are like water leaks in your home. If you catch it early, there is little to fix, repair, or clean up. The longer you wait, the more the damage spreads. Whenever something is significant enough to give either of us discomfort, we bring it up right away while the issue is small, rather than wait until resentment has built up.

In early 2018, I received the opportunity to do the work I love, but it would take me away from Hawaii for a contract term that is a year or two long. There would be opportunities to come home every three weeks or so and I would also have the chance to have Lisa visit me. We discussed the issue in depth and with potential pros and cons. Lisa blessed the idea for me to pursue it, but after a few weeks, it seemed like a subject that she did not want to talk about and I could tell it was giving her some discomfort. While it was just a possibility (in other words, still small), I pushed her to tell me exactly how she felt about it. It was then pretty clear that she thought it would negatively affect our relationship not to spend time in the same space every day. We managed to fix that one while it was still a tiny leak. No commitments had been made, no harm came to anyone, and no penalties were issued.

I could see that her intuition was likely correct and even something like my job was not big enough to jeopardize our relationship. The residual pain from her past relationships popped up, and she did not want to discourage anything I was thinking or doing for fear that I would be mad at her. It was far from the case. I was glad she trusted me enough to tell me the truth, and we could resolve that conflict lovingly and fruitfully.

Fight Fair

Some things are just off limits. If you decide the relationship is more important than the issue, then there is no using the divorce card. Sometimes people use the threat of divorce as a trump to force the other party to concede. That's not fair.

Another thing that is not fair is to bring up a known soft spot or weakness. Everybody has them. Everybody has done something in their life that they are not proud of, feel guilty about, and are ashamed of doing. Whatever the soft spot is, it is off limits. Bringing up these things is a selfish choice made to hurt your partner. You are partners, not competitors. You are in this together; act like it.

Pamela would bring up issues when she felt it was best for her to discuss them, but not necessarily when it was the best time for positive results. She thought it was important to address a situation the moment she thought of it. There were no ground rules, no regard to who might be around, no thought of an opportune time. We had tried to put rules in place, but they never stuck. They were good ideas that were given by experts, but old habits die hard, and high emotions on both sides would usually overrun the rules. The trick is you have to force yourself (NOT the other person) to play by the rules.

One of the best rules to put in place is to pick a time and place to have a discussion. I hated fighting with Pamela in front of the kids, particularly when there would be no resolution. Pick a time when you can focus and choose a space that you find peaceful. I like to look at it this way: If your everyday life is a peaceful and harmonious body of water, the issue is a ripple in the water disrupting to the norm. Your job is to get the relationship back to a peaceful, harmonious place.

If you pick a time and place conducive to a nice conversation, it's likely the emotional aspects of the discussion will dissipate and you will be left to contend with just the issue at hand.

One suggestion: do not pick a time just before bed. If you don't know how long a discussion will take, don't start when you will be tired and cannot continue. Keep in mind that sleep is essential. If an argument does break out just before bed, be okay with going to sleep without resolving it. Also, don't argue when one of you is drunk or otherwise incapacitated. Whatever message you wanted to make is not getting in there.

Lisa and I have had little history of arguing, probably because the issues we have encountered were never more important than our relationship itself. There is a sharing of real feelings and a sincere attempt to understand the other person's point of view. Some ground rules for discussing difficult issues we think are important are hardly different from those you would have with anyone where the relationship is more important than the issue you are dealing with. Here are a few more rules we have to fight as fairly as we can.

Keep calm. You see the shirts and stickers all around town, *Keep Calm and Drink Coffee, Keep Calm and Stay Strong, Keep Calm and Surf,* etc. The sentiment is true in arguing. There is an emotional element to arguing when someone feels something so strongly that they think they need to assert themselves. But no matter what, be calm, rational, and polite. Avoid the escalation that leads to yelling, name-calling, profanity, and everything worse. If things escalate, take a break. Respect that the other person might be overwhelmed and let the break happen. Just make sure to pick a time and place sometime later to resume the specific discussion.

Stick to the issue. If your relationship is worth it, then every threat or issue should be addressed, and each issue that has a real potential to damaging the relationship should be handled separately. I have often been involved in arguments when we started arguing about one issue, but so many unrelated things were brought up that I wasn't sure we were talking about the same issue anymore. Discussing multiple issues at the same time can get confusing and, more often than not, hurts the productivity of the conversation.

Keep your perspective yours. Define things as you see them in your world, not in the world of the person you are arguing with. What I mean by that is talk about how you see the issue, not how your partner sees it. When you impose your thoughts on your partner's point of view, it may feel like an attack and often throws up a defensive wall that makes a compromise (or conclusion) much more difficult. If you describe the issue in terms of how it affects you or others, that does several things. First, it forces you to explore your feelings and positions to validate to yourself that there is something worth bringing up. Second, it gives the other person the chance to hear you and review for himself or herself your differing views of the issue. Try using statements such as "I feel..." as opposed to "You are..." Focus on your perspective and acknowledge that your partner may not share it.

Last, *don't rush to an answer.* Know there are few absolute rights and wrongs and being right is not the goal, anyway. The goal is to understand as kindly and compassionately as you can. Take as much time as you need to find a resolution lovingly.

Prioritize Your Partner's Happiness

Selfishness is one of the biggest threats to creating a relationship that is close and strong. There has to be a self-sacrificing desire to understand the inner workings of your partner in a deep and meaningful way. How your partner thinks, their likes and dislikes, and your concern for their well-being all have to be part of your recipe for creating a healthy relationship. Put your partner's happiness first. Ask yourself this question: How can I make my partner so happy that they would never, ever, ever want to be anywhere but by my side?

Happiness is a way of life, not a destination. Your happiness should be making your spouse's life secure, happy, and positive. You should strive to make your partner look forward to a future with you by their side; it's the best perspective you can give your partner about your relationship. There is little thought of yourself in that perspective, but there may be nothing so rewarding in your life. If you can bridle your self-centered tendencies, and instead focus on your partner's happiness, many issues will melt away in favor of the harmony of the relationship.

Chapter Five

Build Trust

The basis of any and every relationship is some level of trust. Things start out small—the little white lie, hesitance to let your partner look at your phone—simple things. Little walls get built along the way and continue to grow. As the relationship begins to show cracks, trust levels diminish accordingly. As trust declines, the deterioration of the relationship escalates, and the cycle spirals downward. Those relationships will eventually end in disaster and chaos if you do not find ways to build back that trust.

If I honestly look for the beginning of the diminishing trust in my marriage with Pamela, it probably started before we were married. I could not trust my honest feelings with Pamela, but it took quite some time for me to realize it and quite a bit longer for me to realize that was a problem. Once that kind of trust slips from your grasp, it is very hard to regain.

Below are some ways Lisa and I have intentionally reinforced our mutual trust to prevent that from happening.

Be Vulnerable

One of the most trusting things you can do is to open yourself up to your partner, making it safe for them to express their innermost thoughts and feelings to you. Bare it all; show them your weaknesses, your opinions, your unpopular thoughts, your bad habits—not just the strengths everybody loves to show. Lisa and I have found that the more we know about each other's weaknesses, the more we want to support each other.

This is not necessarily what happens in all cases or even in most cases. Most people struggle with being vulnerable; it is not the way in our society. We put up fronts and facades to hide who we are or how we are doing, social media being only a single example of that. But even still, no one likes to bare their wounds or weaknesses, even if it is in a safe place. In some cases being vulnerable leads to the other person walking away (or running away depending on the case), causing you hurt, pain, and suffering.

Being vulnerable is being true to yourself and the other person. It is the only way to build a loving, trusting relationship where the other person will have your back if you fail. For us, we explore each other's thoughts regularly and seek to understand every bit of the other person. We do this so we can support each other where we need support and relish the other person's victories as if we were in their shoes. I love that about our relationship.

Lisa has an irrational fear of lizards. It makes little sense, and Lisa knows it. Often people will snicker or giggle when she jumps away from the small creatures, but I know to her it is as serious as a heart attack. Instead of ridiculing her for it, I have taken the position to protect her from lizards whenever they come up. It is the least I can do for her, and I can do it because I understand her vulnerabilities, because she trusted me with them.

On a more serious note, we had to be deeply open with each other when we discussed whether I would take the job where I would be away from home most of the time. In a safe and calm space, where we could talk without it escalating, we were vulnerable with each other, trusting that we would not be attacked. The conclusion was clear; this opportunity was not right for our relationship. Lisa asked me if I was upset with her, but I told her it was quite the opposite. I was glad she felt safe enough to say what she was thinking. That is precisely what vulnerability working through trust looks like.

Before I found Lisa, I can safely say I was not vulnerable to anyone. That was not an active choice, but rather a thick skin that grew over a long time—probably since I was a kid.

Regarding vulnerability, I learned early on that my feelings of insecurity, doubt, and lack of confidence were bad things that should be squelched, overcome, and then discarded. I remember in Little League I was scared of getting hit by the ball and could barely keep my eyes open when a pitch came my way. I had been hit by the ball once or twice before, and it hurt, so I was terrified of batting. The fear was never addressed. My parents (and I) thought I would get better if I practiced, but the more practice I got, the more I practiced the fear of getting hit. I played one season and then never played again, thus never having to deal with that insecurity again. That was my method: drop anything that brought out my insecurities. This applied to relationships, too. Relationships with girlfriends rarely passed the two-month mark because I could not open up to them. They would pry into my personality and want to know me better, but I would feel vulnerable and get out fast. I would do whatever it took to sabotage the relationship to keep my faults and shortcomings to myself.

I built a wall around me to fence in my vulnerabilities. Forty-plus years' worth of hiding and barricading is not good ground for a trusting relationship. That's why I knew that I had to make strides in this area with my relationship with Lisa. Luckily, Lisa is fantastic at "listening to understand," rather than "listening to respond." I gave her what I was feeling little bits at a time as a way to test the waters, and each time we went through that exercise, I found I was in a safe place with her. It was okay for me to include her in my exploration of my feelings and, in fact, sharing helped me figure things out better than before! I cared about her feelings as well. When she was bothered by something, I made sure I was a safe outlet for honest discussions.

Over years of continuing to improve in this area, I have built up a comfortable amount of trust with Lisa. I know she will consistently take care of me and my feelings and I will do the same for her. We are vulnerable, perhaps to a fault, but that has brought us closer together than either of us had experienced.

Be Intimate

The intimacy I am discussing ranges in behavior from a touch on the shoulder to passionate sex. It is a mutually agreeable and desired kind of intimacy that feels good with your partner but is weird with other people. There is a special version of touch that should be reserved for married couples and sex is only part of that equation. This kind of touch is not forced by either party, and both people desire the action and feel completely safe. If you do not feel safe or don't want to be part of the behavior, that should be considered abuse and is cause for alarm no matter how you cut it.

Lisa and I enjoy being intimate with each other whatever the action is. It's not just about sex, but about other things like holding hands when we are walking around the mall. We like sitting on the same side of the table and gazing into each other's eyes as we talk. There are many similar things we consider intimate, things that build our intimacy and trust with each other in little ways. We don't do those things with anyone else, and we don't take our intimacy or closeness for granted.

Our strategy is to employ whatever behaviors bring us closer together and let them happen naturally. Try it! If you try something and don't like it, that's fine! Simply don't do it again. Just know there is a lot of vulnerability involved in pursuing intimacy that continually requires trust.

Let's Talk about Infidelity

I have skirted an issue that is prevalent in our society and thus something we have to discuss. We could debate what defines infidelity, but it all boils down to the desire to venture outside of the relationship.

Where does this desire stem from? I agree with what people say about wanting adventure, excitement, and variety when a marriage is dull, boring, and uneventful. Marriage, they claim, is encumbered with tons of things like responsibility, structure, and expectations. They also claim an obvious lack of excitement. The craving to seek intimate relationships outside of the marriage fulfills that feeling of excitement—when chills run down your spine and raise the hairs on your neck. We are emotional beings that need that kind of thing as much as we need stability. But believe me, an affair is not the only way to bring excitement into a stable, static marriage. We have to make time in our lives for our hobbies and things that are fun. When we don't create space for the things we desire to do, we develop a hole in our life that eventually evokes actions that are out of character.

I am no stranger to either side of the infidelity equation. When I was on the adventure side of it, I felt great; when I was in the world of stability, I felt guilty and ashamed. When I was on the victim side of the equation, it was impossible for me to keep feelings of inadequacy from rising up and eating away at me from the inside out. My own emotions were the highest of the highs and lowest of the lows. I could always feel this duality.

I believe the key is balancing the times you have stability in your life and when you have adventure in your life. If you spend time in the stable world doing responsible things, you should carve out time to have fun, enjoy life, adventure, and do whatever you want.

The way Lisa and I deal with that is we spend time in both worlds. We set in motion things that will make us feel secure in our lives, and then (almost equally) do things just for fun and excitement. We'll go on our little adventures to try new things all the time, and most of those things are NOT sexual. New experiences keep life exciting, and any desire to share those experiences with someone outside of our relationship is completely nullified by doing them together. I recently heard someone talk about how the world accepts relationships breaking up as easily as they start. It seems we have adopted the position that jumping ship from relationship to relationship is normal. Well, our solution is to continually renew the excitement and fun in our relationship.

Be Communicative

There is nothing we keep from each other. Well, I take that back. I didn't tell Lisa about the surprise party I threw for her, but that is about it. We have no reservations about telling our partner anything and everything.

When I first met Pamela, I told her everything. We had a clean slate, and it was easy to be open with one another. We were also just learning about each other, so there were guards in place that we were trying to soften so we could get to know each other. As time passed, when I presented my thoughts Pamela would sometimes judge or dismiss them, which slowly ate away at our bond. And I did the same to her. We each created a mental list of items not to discuss. As that became the new norm. My list kept growing and growing until larger issues were placed on the list. Soon, there were just as many things I wasn't telling her as things I brought up. The theme here is the small things snowball. So communicate about everything, especially the small things.

Lisa and I are a solid team. She makes me a better person, and I rely on her for perspective and guidance, especially her expertise in dealing with people. There is synergy in our relationship, where 1+1 equals way more than 2. Because I believe this fact with all my heart, we talk about everything. Nothing is off limits. When there is an uncomfortable topic that feels like it could put a wedge between us, we make it a special point to address it at the earliest moment. Those conversations used to be more difficult, but they get easier. Like a muscle, the more you use it, the stronger the skill becomes.

As an example, this morning I felt the need to apologize for inviting people over last minute yesterday evening. Lisa took it in stride, but I felt bad for not asking her first. In my previous marriage, that would have been a disaster. Still, in our discussion this morning, it was good for me to clear the air and find that there were no adverse feelings or resentment.

On another occasion, Lisa was feeling uncomfortable with a friendship I had with a woman. I thought it was platonic, but Lisa felt that there was more there. At this point, Lisa and I were in a committed relationship and were open and honest about everything, but we still dealt with our own residual hurt. She shared her concerns and her insights, letting her guard down as we discussed the issue until we were satisfied that each of us had been heard. We tested her theory and found that she was right and I was blind to it! After this, I was convinced that Lisa and I, as a team, are better at finding each other's blind spots than we are alone. Our relationship strengthened because we listened and opened up to each other. Communication is crucial to restoring trust issues.

Chapter Six

Connection, Connection, Connection

By virtue of living in the physical world, our existence is bound by time and space. Those two things connect us. In a relationship between two people, there must be a desire to have that connection by being together, whether that is physically or mentally. Sharing our time in the same space is not always easy, but it is worth the reward.

Time Spent Together and Time Spent Apart

Because we found each other a little later in life, Lisa and I want to spend as much time together as possible before we depart this Earth. In our case, all of our children are grown, so our empty nest helps us have time to spend together. I know with all the busyness children bring, it is often easiest for one parent to take one child to soccer practice while the other parent takes the other kid to art class. This strategy is efficient, but not altogether good for building your relationship. It is especially important in those situations that you set aside time to spend together as a couple. This is difficult, but it is necessary.

Think of the couples that have medical challenges affect the amount of future they have together. Nothing for them is as valuable as time. This is a superb perspective for everyone to have. Once you have created a loving and happy relationship, you learn to cherish every moment you have together. For all of us, the time we have together is unknown. Lisa and I want to protect our future together so much that we take preventative measures, too, like dieting, exercise, and other things that will keep us well and elongate our future.

As an aside, having a desire for the well-being of your partner will, by itself, extend your time together. When Lisa and I first got together, we wanted to spend every minute together. Sometimes this meant skipping a daily workout routine, and then it often meant that. In our efforts to spend time together, we harmed each other. Through our discussions, we knew this lifestyle was unsustainable. We changed our habits to schedule in workouts and be together at the same time. I know I look silly doing Lisa's girlie workouts, but they kick my butt! We now go to the gym four to six times a week. On weekdays, we're in the gym at 4:00 in the morning. We make healthy food choices whenever we can without suppressing dinners out and gatherings with friends, as those connections are necessary. We regularly see our doctors. We have put insurance in place to make sure the other one is taken care of should something catastrophic happen. This kind of attention pours out of a healthy relationship, with all its benefits to boot!

We also try to minimize the time spent apart, cutting it down to regular work hours only. This works wonders. Even when one of you has unusual events (doctor appointments, critical business meetings, etc.), make it a point, if possible, to join the other one during those times. The other person's issues are ultimately important to you, too.

Chronic time apart is both a symptom and a self-perpetuating problem. Once you have an unhealthy amount of time spent alone, it encourages a breakdown in communication, which will make you want to spend less time together.

In my first marriage, there were natural things that kept the time we spent together limited. We enjoyed different hobbies, took separate roles in raising the kids, and we had different friends, just to name a few. As the relationship struggled, we leaned toward those things that made us feel good, like different hobbies and friends. Soon we spent more time separated by those things and it affected our desire to spend time together. This was a silent killer that crept up on us over time; the longer it goes, the worse it gets, but there was no tangible indication it was happening. This is another example of an issue left unchecked that spiraled out of control.

In my relationship with Lisa, we still have hobbies that are different, but we each have taken on some favorite hobbies and interests of the other person. Lisa has attempted to take on motorcycle riding, but still prefers to sit in the backseat of my motorcycle than ride her own. I have taken on cycling and swimming, which Lisa likes to do, so we can spend more time together. Ninety percent of the time, we grocery shop together and spend every available moment together, even if we're doing different things. We make it a point to minimize time apart because every minute counts.

Sharing Space and Comfortable Silence

Most couples will have things to do that only apply to one partner. Non-working time and evenings are often filled with individual tasks, personal hobbies, and other interests. The idea is to make sure those individual interests don't keep you apart. The easiest way to do so is to make it a point to be in the same space while doing your things.

Though it is important for you to accomplish tasks, it is at least as equally important for you to have that connection with each other, even if that only means being able to see or hear each other typing on the computer. We've found it's the small things that enhance our enjoyment of the time we spend together. Clearly, when you are engaged with each other in a deep conversation or working on a problem together, you enjoy those times, but the quiet times can also bring you happiness and great satisfaction.

When you enjoy being in the same space with no conversation or any active interaction, you can sense peace—in the room and in the relationship. Happy couples are ok to sit next to each other and work on separate things, or watch TV, or cook different things in the kitchen, so long as they are together. It doesn't mean that there is nothing to say, or that there is any negative emotion. The silence does not bother them.

My first marriage started out with this ability. Pamela and I could just spend some time together in casual or no conversation. But later, as we chose to spend more time apart, time together was always under a certain level of constraint that required that we have a "talk" about a serious issue in our relationship. The problem of not spending enough time together developed, by our own choices, so the time we spent together could not be spent casually or quietly in the same space. I didn't see that how we handled our time was becoming a larger and larger problem, but now, having been through it, I am very aware of it with Lisa.

Sometimes I will help Lisa set up her classroom or grade multiple-choice tests, understanding that I am diminishing her workload so we can spend more time together. I try to do that as much as I can because the time we spend together is the most valuable thing we have. As I write this paragraph, Lisa is working on a project she needs to have ready for her classroom while I am on my laptop. We are doing two separate things with no conversation, and yet we are less than 10 feet apart. These moments are essential to us.

Create Your Shared Morning Routine

In this time of personal growth, I am finding myself drawn to any ideas that further personal development. One of the significant catch phrases in this area is morning routines—also known as priming, kick-starting, or "the miracle morning." Apparently, almost all the world's most impactful people have some morning routine. This immediately sparked an interest in me to see if a morning routine made any difference in my life.

Previously, I had little (if any) routine at all. I take that back; I had the "drive the kids to school" routine for more than a dozen years. I would wake up with just enough time to brush my teeth and take a shower before I needed to get the kids up and get them ready to go. I loved, loved, loved the hour drive into town with just the girls and me, a time where we could just talk and enjoy each other's company. Once the girls were dropped off at school, my workday began with phone calls to all my supervisors, and on from there. My typical mornings were a little chaotic.

Life now is different for many reasons, the biggest being that the kids are now all adults and don't take up any of my mornings. I have realized that now is my time to create new habits, one of them being my morning routine.

Our regular weekday mornings are standardized with little to do except follow the protocol we have set up. Lisa wakes up at 3:30 AM and gets ready for the gym. I wake up at 3:50 AM (it doesn't take me as long to get ready), and we are out of the door at 4:00 AM. Lisa's routine at the gym lasts an hour while I put in 30 to 40 minutes and then meditate while I wait for Lisa. Once we're home, we shower and get ready for work, and I finish the rest of my routine.

What remains of my morning ritual follows the *Miracle Morning* routine developed by my friend and mentor Hal Elrod. He designed it based on what the most successful people in the world do. He found out they shared a few morning habits: meditating, journaling, visualizations, affirmations, exercise, and reading. His theory was if one or two of these things were good, shouldn't all six every morning be better? He created an acronym for doing all six things and called it SAVERS: for silence (meditation), affirmations, visualizations, exercise, reading, and scribing (journaling).

So, having checked exercise and meditation off the list, I pick up where I left off—affirmations. I have a document I store in the cloud that records my statements of who I am, what my strengths are, and the general focus of my life. I read them out loud to myself. Sometimes I update the affirmations to fit any changes to my current perspective. Sometimes I add affirmations in, and sometimes I take some off. The point is to remind me of what's important to me, my purpose in life, who I am, and what I can do.

Once I have finished that, I jump to visualizations. I have a similar document for this that I re-read every morning. My visualizations focus on our goals, such as traveling to parts of the world that we have not seen. They also focus on goals for what kind of person I would like to become. I have a Pinterest board where I have saved many things I would love to experience. The visual aspect of Pinterest is useful because pictures help shape my focus for my goals. I have often heard if you can't visualize your destination, you will never create a path to get there.

Once I get through my visualization, I do a little writing. I use an app called Grid Diary in which I have created a standard template that prompts me with a question. The questions I ask myself are: What am I grateful for? Who do I want to be today? What is the one thing I must do to make my relationships so strong and enjoyable that they become unbreakable? What one thing must I do at work such that other things become easier or unnecessary? What is the one thing I must do today to reach my current business goal? What is the story I tell myself that will guide my day? This time of reflection is fruitful for having a self-aware day where you can grow.

The last step of my morning routine is reading. This step, unfortunately, gets eliminated on some mornings when I am rushed, but it is vital to continue to learn. Most of the books that interest me are about personal development, which helps me grow a lot, but your choice can be about anything that would interest you!

At the end of my morning routine, I feel refreshed and ready to go, already knowing what I need to accomplish for the day. It gives me an edge starting the day with clarity and motivation and feels amazing.

By living out my purpose to be the best husband and partner to Lisa, everything else in my life needs to support that purpose, including writing this book. My morning routine is part of how I live out that purpose. I have focused my efforts in my morning routine to reinforce my goal of being the best husband and partner. This way, every morning starts with propelling me in that direction. Living with a purpose makes every decision easier to make and morning routines focus every decision in the right direction from the moment your day begins.

Travel Together

One of the best parts of being in a relationship is traveling together and experiencing new things. Traveling in my first marriage was something we looked forward to at the beginning, but our flaw was that we expected it always to go as planned. As trip dates got closer, anticipating every problem would heighten the level of stress until the trip was more of a burden than an adventure. Trips would focus on avoiding pitfalls rather than enjoying the experience we had planned. This was not enjoyable; in fact, it was tiring.

Traveling is something Lisa and I look forward to each time we have the opportunity. If we could travel all year long, I'd imagine that we would have no problems in our relationship at all. But alas, like most couples, that is not a luxury we have. But we try to fulfill the purpose of each trip and also do some additional fun things together. The key is that we talk about as much as we can beforehand. We plan ahead and check in with each other during the planning process to make sure we are coming on the trip from the same team. Once we are on the trip, we maintain a flexible schedule, so when we encounter something cool and unexpected, we can be spontaneous and have an experience we didn't plan. Usually, that becomes part of the highlight reel of the trip.

If there's anywhere that life will throw you a curve ball, it's traveling. We've learned to not lose our minds over changing the plans mid-trip. Our relationship is an experience more valuable and important than anything we may have missed.

Chapter Seven

Attitude is Truly Everything

If fixing problems is like knocking over dominos, the first domino you should concentrate on it is having the right attitude toward your relationship. Tackling that problem will make the remaining dominos topple. New challenges will always come your way, so developing and maintaining the attitude that the relationship you have is worthwhile and worth working for will fortify you. Other ways to adjust your attitude include acting with courtesy, practicing gratitude, and using meditation to understand your inner workings.

Behaving with Courtesy

It seems entirely intuitive to treat your partner with courtesy, but in the reality of day-to-day life, common courtesies are not so common after all. Affording each other the courtesy you would give someone you deeply respect and honor is the goal. Once you can do that, your relationship will move toward amazing.

Many romantic relationships start out great in terms of everyday courtesy, but these fall off as time goes on. That's exactly what happened in my marriage with Pamela. As our value to each other diminished, so did our care to have a courteous relationship. It became clear that there was a lesser expectation to be polite. What bugs me is that our society says that's okay! We joke about relationships and make fun of marriages. Some so many people can easily relate to the ridicule that marriages are a comedian's playground, fodder for entertainment. I, for one, am not entertained. This and the windy relationships of the celebrity world normalize bad relationships. It upsets me to see this when good relationships should be the norm and bad relationships should be the exception. This is where I hope I can have some influence. Whether it be familiarity, resentment, or any number of bad circumstances that cause this shift in courtesy, it is a long road back. So be proactive! The rules we learned as children still apply:

- Be polite.
- Always say please and thank you.
- Don't interrupt when someone else is talking.
- Open/hold doors for others.
- Offer the first choice to others.
- Say "Excuse me" to get someone's attention.

I make it a habit of doing all of those things because it makes Lisa feel special, and to me, she is incredibly special.

Have an Attitude of Gratitude

Gratitude is the essential attitude to adopt for a good relationship and a good life. With gratitude in place, every thought about your relationship is focused on what is already good and what would make the relationship better.

In my first marriage, I wasn't grateful for Pamela's willingness to stick it out with me. And I certainly felt taken for granted for my persistence to stay together. There were many times I felt this way, and I am sure she felt the same. These small instances built up, bit by bit, a wall of disdain when we could have had a sea of gratitude.

Lisa and I practice gratitude when we think of how thankful we are for the opportunity to create our relationship. We are so grateful for each other, not just for the one-in-a-million chance to meet, but for the effort we put into taking care of each other, nurturing our relationship, and bending our lives around each other through acceptance for our differences and similarities.

Here's one easy thing to be thankful about: If you are reading this, you can thank your lucky stars because your lifestyle is probably in the top 1% of people in the world. Crazy, but it's probably true. These relational problems have little magnitude compared to areas of the world that are war-torn, are overpopulated, have high rates of starvation, or have no clean water. How often are we unsure when our next meal will come? Sure, relational issues are important, but if you keep them in perspective with you not having to fight for survival, it is easier for your default attitude to be gratefulness.

One way you can live your gratitude is through service to others, even to people other than your partner. Doing things for people who need the help not only feels good, but it's also the right thing to do. One way I do this is through the Rotary Club. Helping people accomplish things they could not achieve for themselves, with no desire for anything in return, makes you feel so good inside, and you want more of it. It was also amazing to find people so devoted to making the world a better place.

I reveal this part of my life not to pat myself on the back; far from it. During those years spent in the service of Rotary, I got the opportunity to see the world from a different perspective. It was in those times I honestly felt like I had no problems at all that could compare with the trouble that some of those folks we were helping had. This kind of volunteerism quickly creates gratitude for the blessing of your situation. The feeling of gratitude in this context also motivates me to continue to serve other people who are less fortunate than I am.

Attitude Check—Meditation

Often during times of high stress, especially stress in your relationship, our minds become a scramble of a thousand different thoughts. I know when I had the issues of my company closing and the impending divorce negotiations, my mind was shot. There were so many things fighting their way to the forefront of my mind that there were days on end when I could not sleep. Other times, my efforts to think through a single issue were thwarted because I could not concentrate on one thing for any sustained time. This would have been an opportune time to have adopted the practice of meditation, had I only known its benefits.

All my best ideas come out of times when things are quiet around me. The best way I can make this happen is through meditation. I meditate every day. When I am in a noisy surrounding, as I am in the morning waiting for Lisa to finish her workout, I will sit with my eyes closed, with headphones in but nothing playing, so people will not bother me. I can sense their presence, but can quickly dismiss the sensation and return to my thoughts.

During these times of meditation, I set an intention to improve something. More often than not, it is to grow one of my relationships. My first step is to visualize the ideal relationship. I then use all of my senses to develop a realistic world in my mind of how that relationship would be, with as much detail as I can imagine about what it would look like, sound like, feel like, smell like, and taste like. Then, I break it down into manageable parts, for example, a single morning greeting. Then I can see how that part differs from how my relationship already is and create a path of getting from here to there. My thinking is that by taking little steps in the right direction, all the sections will compile to form the relationship I'm looking for.

For example, between Lisa and I, my visualization goes through a day together. We wake up when the sun comes up and get dressed for the gym or a run through the neighborhood. I imagine the conversation we will have while we are getting our exercise. I envision the crisp air on our skin and the sound of our feet as they hit the pavement. I imagine the hot shower and the feel of clean, loose-fitting clothes as we discuss the things we want to get accomplished that day. We decide on the menu for breakfast, whether it be a vegetable smoothie or some fruit. Perhaps it's a special day, and we want to go out for pancakes with macadamia *haupia* cream sauce or maybe eggs benedict. I imagine us working side by side on the sofa or perhaps across from each other at the dining room table, allowing comfortable silence to envelop the room. I can see the water bottle near Lisa's computer and my favorite stainless-steel cup filled with watered-down iced tea with three lemon wedges. I can hear the ice cubes in the cup jingle as they collide with the side of the cup while I take a sip. I imagine we break midday for a snack or lunch. We talk about the interactions we may have had with people on the phone in the morning and what news there is in our family. We think about our plans for the evening, whether it be a quiet evening at home, or perhaps a semi-elaborate dinner we put together ourselves, or maybe it's a good time to get together with another couple to catch up. I go through each scenario with as much detail as I can to cement that this WILL BE the reality we develop.

I look at the detail of that ideal reality and match it up with our current reality. I pick an item and determine what I need to do to get from here to there. For example, the favorite stainless-steel cup is something I already have; there is nothing for me to do there. We both still have jobs that prevent us from seeing each other. Lots of work to do there. Lisa retires in four years, so I need to figure out how to retire in four years, too, and determine how we would sustain our lifestyle after that point. There's more work to do to create that path.

The imagination works so quickly. Using it during meditation is a powerful tool. Imagine a perfectly average day. What does it look like, smell like, taste like? How are you feeling? What are you wearing, and what's on your schedule? Take an inventory of that perfect day and compare it to your average day now. What are the similarities and the differences? How do you make today's differences become the ideal things you identified in your dreams? How will you feel when you get that discrepancy to match your ideal thing? Will you feel closer to your goal? I hope you, like me, can say yes.

Chapter Eight

Commit Like You Mean It

Because of my bad habits in relationships when I was younger, friends of mine would refer to my girlfriends as furniture. A terrible analogy, but it was fitting. Once there was a little wear and tear on the couch, as the analogy goes, I would move it out and bring in a new one. Even my first wife would jokingly refer to herself as furniture. Looking back at that now, it was dumb to continue to view things that way, but being young and stupid, I did not know better. I did not understand what real commitment looks like.

When I say commitment, I mean committing to your partner fully, putting the relationship above all else. Supporting each other with more than just money—with your entire lives. Encouraging each other to grow and develop. Envisioning who you will be together. This doesn't mean you lose yourself, but rather that your two futures become one future together, and that's how you want it to be.

Commitment

You need to make an affirmative decision to commit to continuous improvement in every facet of your relationship. That decision to invest in each other and the well-being of the relationship is the first strategy you need.

I am committed to Lisa. She is my primary relationship, even above the relationship I have with my children, believe it or not. She is the priority in my life. We both feel this way about each other, and that provides us a sense of confidence and security in our relationship.

Similarly but separately, I am committed to the relationship between us. It sounds like the same thing, but it is different. The relationship we have is significant to me. Making it strong and healthy also is a priority. The thoughts and behaviors that go into improving the relationship differ from the things I need to do, or Lisa needs to do, to improve ourselves. We need to commit to both.

Promote Your Partner

One of the dearest things to a spouse's ear is when our partner compliments any aspect of who we are as a person. I take any opportunity I get to tell people how wonderful my wife is. Occasionally, she is nearby and overhears my conversation. She knows, without a doubt, that she enamors me, and I adore and respect her for the things she does and the person she is. Conversely, the compliments I overhear my wife giving me always bring an inner smile, knowing she appreciates me and revels in me.

We promote the good traits of each other at every opportunity, even to each other, ALL THE TIME. We regularly verbalize the good of our partner, and soon we internalize the praise we receive.

It's a crazy wonderful thing. It can fix esteem issues and insecurities and can give your partner full assurance that you support and believe in them.

One principle that comes to mind when I think about promoting Lisa comes from Dave Kekich's Credos, which says you are constantly growing or shrinking; there is no standing still. If you are not promoting the goodness of your partner at every opportunity, you are, in fact, diminishing how you value your partner. This is my belief.

Respect Each Other's Individuality

We have been talking about so far has concentrated on the couple and the relationship. It is a single thing, yet it comprises two people with individual talents, skills, desires, needs, etc. Regardless of how we make the relationship better and closer, we must maintain our individuality, too. It is the gift you bring to the party.

In my first marriage, Pamela and I led individual lives—too individual, in fact, as you have already seen. Lisa and I, on the other hand, are very similar and spend tons of time together. But we have also been able to keep our own interests. Lisa is very interested in health and wellness. She enjoys meal planning, exercise planning, and learning about wellness to live a long and fruitful life. She does this for both of us, but she is the one who creates the plan. That is her thing. On the opposite end, I love learning music, perfecting my voice, interpreting songs in a certain way to convey the message the way I want people to receive it. I even sing in a barbershop quartet, which I find fun and challenging. I do it at the hobby level, so it is purely for my enjoyment. Barbershopping (do you like how I turned that into a verb?) is my thing.

These individual things shape who we are and give us the perspective we bring to the relationship. They provide us the ability to have a differing opinion. We are different, but on a team, we can be more than just two individuals. I like to think of it as an enhanced sounding board. A typical sounding board just bounces back to you what was said, without inflection or comment. An enhanced sounding board takes the information given, processes it, and potentially gives it back to you with a different interpretation or meaning. We know differing from each other is a positive thing. We are more than the sum of our parts because we make each other grow every time we bring our individualities together.

We put this into practice especially when I am emotionally charged, and I need to write someone a letter or note. I know I can't produce the best work when I'm angry, so I have Lisa read it to get her opinion if the note is clear and considerate or not. She brings to the table something different than I do, and we have enough trust in our relationship to be honest about how well or poorly I performed in writing that emotionally charged piece. The outcome is so much better for having both perspectives.

Plan for the Future

One of the exciting things about being married is envisioning your future together. Where do you both want to be?

Unfortunately, I did this poorly in my first marriage. I included Pamela in my vision… I just did not tell her about it, nor did I ask for hers. I thought it was a good plan we could both live with, but she was not part of the discussion. I haphazardly brought her into the conversation at different times during the process, but never consulted her on what the plan would be. I brought her along for the ride. This is not the way to build a future together or to show your partner you are committed to them.

In my marriage with Lisa, we regularly review our joint vision and our plan to live a long and fruitful life together. We discuss what it looks like, what it smells like, what it sounds like, and especially how it feels. We talk with detail regarding our hopes and our dreams to make them as real as possible. It makes us excited to get our intermediate goals achieved so we can see that our plans are playing out the way we wanted and our vision is becoming a reality. Our commitment to each other allows for this kind of progress as we work toward our future together.

Chapter Nine

LoveLife FAQs

Since I love to talk about my relationship with Lisa, I get a lot of questions about how to handle the transition out of a bad one. This section answers the most common ones we hear in our groups and seminars, and even from our friends.

One thing to keep in mind: dealing with your ex is always tricky, but it is so much better when you handle it together with your new partner. When Lisa and I first got together, calling ourselves a team was one of the love-struck things we did. It was cutesy at first, but it soon became a fundamental trait of our relationship. It put us on the same side against anything that would try to separate us. At first, we used it to play defense against those who did not support our relationship, but later we realized it was also useful for defending each other against our residual hurt—from within and from our exes. After all, if you are a team, your relationship is so much more significant than any amount of residual hurt you have to endure. Be sure you tackle these hard interactions as a team.

How do I keep my ex from getting under my skin?

Ex-spouses are talented at pushing your buttons, especially since they had years of practice when you were married. Lisa and I make sure we talk about how our exes affect us so we can help each other diminish the effects of their words or actions. Identifying what they want and what buttons they will push to get it gives us tools to stop any pain they may cause.

Another strategy for combatting button-pushing is interacting on your terms, not your ex's. For example, it used to be that one of our exes would want to meet immediately to discuss something. Almost always, the matter was never as urgent as our exes made things out to be. Lisa and I knew that interacting with them under their conditions would put us in an environment that would make it easy to fall into our same habits from the old relationship. What we would do instead is schedule the phone call on our schedule, or, if it were a meeting, choose a public location where we could guarantee civil behavior on both sides. If possible, we would schedule another meeting or phone call right after it to limit the time we gave to our ex. After all, that relationship was no longer the top priority.

One important thing to remember is that you have fault in your old relationship, too. Refrain from hurting or manipulating your ex and respect their space. They may have more to work through than you do, so give them time.

How do you talk to your new partner about your past relationship (awkward!)?

One strength of my relationship with Lisa is our ability to talk freely with each other. We can talk to each other about anything and everything. But, it's still awkward when we bring up stories from our past marriages, be they happy or sad.

One thing to be leery of when recounting old stories is their context. I like all the gritty details, but for most cases, it is better only to give the background needed. Be sure that when the story is one of some disaster, the meaning you provide is always framed by your new relationship and its improvements. For example, I told Lisa about I got food poisoning when on my first honeymoon, and the conflict that created. I framed that with how Lisa and I deal well with unexpected occurrences on our trips. Notice, I only told the part of the honeymoon story that was relevant.

On the other end of the spectrum, bringing back a happy experience should make you remember what you are striving for in this relationship. For example, Lisa and I are talking about going on a cruise. Lisa went on a Disney Cruise during her previous marriage, and she has been recounting how they spent their time and the astounding array of food that was always available. Those stories are to help us get excited about planning for a cruise, but we frame that by remembering it will only be one week in our lifetime of happiness.

How do you introduce your new relationship to your kids from your first marriage?

Our kids were all young adults when Lisa and I got together, so there was less drama than there could have been. Either way, what's important is that the children see that the relationship between you and your partner is happy, healthy, loving, and unbreakable. When the children know and feel that you love and care for each other, you have a good starting point. Making your relationship a shining beacon for what a relationship should be will give the older children the comfort that their parent will be taken care of. There may be bumps in the road, so be ready to take as much time as needed and do not have expectations of acceptance. Instead, pour everything you have into loving your partner well, and they will notice.

Remember, however, the decisions you are making affect your children's lives, even when they are adults. Consider them and consider being a good example to them at all times. No one is perfect, so this is especially hard. But if their model for a relationship is healthy, it will bode well for their future relationships.

Also, keep in mind that your progress in your relationship with your partner will transfer to your other relationships. If you learn to be calm with your spouse, you can learn to be calm with your kids. Pursuing your primary relationship will benefit all the other ones in your life.

How do you approach your new spouse's children?

When Lisa and I first started our relationship, we did not let the introductions to other people in our lives be haphazard. We carefully picked the specific time when the children would be introduced to their new step-parent and step-siblings. When possible, we would explain to our children how it was important to us that the children have a good relationship with the new family in their lives because we loved each other so much. Once that set in, the kids were excited to meet the new members of their family, and only then did we make the introductions.

Once we made the initial introductions, Lisa and I understood that we needed to create and maintain individual relationships with each of the kids and let that happen at each child's own pace. It was slow but rewarding to forge those new relationships!

When will this ordeal be over?

When will this pain and suffering be over? Great question. Obviously, that answer is different for everyone. For some people, perhaps it's never. My hope for you is that you get through whatever debilitating hurt you have quickly, moving to a point where you can operate in life normally and objectively look back at the causes of your hurt (even if you were the source). Examining your hurt, its origins, and the residual pain will bring you a lasting resolution to the effects of the past. The analysis takes away any power the hurt has over you. You have everything you need to move past this point in your life.

For me, much of the hurt from my previous relationship stopped right away once I was away from the situation. I once heard this idea about physical pain and muscle soreness: if you work out until you have pain, when you stop the activity that caused the pain and the pain begins to subside, you have fatigue. If, on the other hand, the pain gets worse after you have stopped the culprit activity, you have an injury. I like to think this is similar to what happens with emotional hurt. If the hurt subsides once the situation is removed, perhaps you were just tired of the situation. If the pain gets worse, you have a significant hurt that needs to be worked through.

In my case, I also believe that the hurt was not caused by something I did or believed; it came from the situation I was in. Once that situation ceased to exist, so did the hurt. From then, it took time for the things I hid away to emerge so I could evaluate, prioritize and work on them. Since I had Lisa to help me through my emotional difficulty, the process was thoughtful and caring. We tackled the things that were more severe, and the less impactful items were brought up later. Some things are still being worked on.

In my case, my divorce was paired with closing my company. Residual hurt from the company's demise directly related to my actions or inactions, so there was much more to process. Getting to the point that I could objectively look my role in the relationship with Pamela was perhaps about three to four months after the physical separation from the relationship. To own up to my role in the demise of the company took every bit of a year and a half before I could even look at the individual items objectively and see how my actions were right or wrong and where I could find an improvement in how I handled things. Also, because the company had many moving parts that were all affected differently by actions of mine, things were more complicated to sort out, and since there was no rebound in the company, there was no way to say what worked or what would have been the better choice, either.

One of the things Lisa regularly says when she hears people talk about improving the world for their kids is, why don't people try to improve their kids for the world? In my attempt to improve myself for Lisa and, yes, for the world, too, I try to fix my psychological flaws and incorrect thinking. I have discovered that I have character flaws that were around before I was in any relationship and those still need to be addressed to this day.

This book is an adventure into that self-improvement. I enjoy the process and like who I am becoming and, because I enjoy it, I will continue to try to become a better human for the world.

Chapter Ten

What to Do When the Sh*t Hits the Fan

One of the great things about life is it gives you fantastic opportunities to start fresh every day. No opportunity hits you squarer in between the eyes as the mid-life crisis.

Most people fear the mid-life crisis. After experiencing a mid-life crisis firsthand and witnessing it in friends and others around us, Lisa and I welcome the event, and we think you should, too. It can be a life-changing phenomenon, but more often than not it makes people better than they were before, with more clarity about their life than they ever had.

My mid-life crisis was tumultuous and scary, but it brought about the most profound evaluation of my life that I have ever experienced, and it changed me for the better.

The ordeal lasted several years and it took me a while to realize what it was. There were no obvious changes or big compulsive purchases like a sports car or a new motorcycle—I had had a motorcycle since I was a teenager and had recently sold the Corvette to provide a down payment for a house. The precursor to my life evaluation happened when I was diagnosed with diabetes. A year before my diagnosis, my father had been diagnosed with type 2 diabetes and I tried to be a good son and learn about the disease and be supportive of my father's new journey ahead of him. It was an arm's length transaction, as it was not me; I was invincible. When I was diagnosed, everything changed. I knew a little about the disease because I had done a bit of reading up on the subject, but now it had become my death sentence. Life was suddenly a finite time I had to get things right.

After being diagnosed, I was in a funk that I could not explain, and I felt sorry for myself and wallowed in my misery for a month or two until my logic decided it was time for me to at least find out what was it all about. As I read every bit of information I found and learned more, I crawled out of my misery pit, my knowledge bolstered my confidence, and I looked toward the future with hope. Still, there was the knowledge I was indeed mortal and had an expiration date.

As that expiration date sat in the back of my mind, I planned for the eventuality that I would no longer be here and my children needed to be taken care of. I worked harder than ever to make sure everything was in place to take care of all of my obligations. During this season of my life, I experienced the commencement of my mid-life crisis: a trip to Kauai.

A trip to Kauai? Your life blew up in a tropical paradise? Well, no, not really, but it's where the wheels in my mind first turned. A good buddy of mine was getting married on Kauai, and although I had buried myself in work, he was (and is) an important friend of mine and I would not miss that wedding for anything. It was a five-day vacation, with a paddle trip down the Napali coast and a weekend wedding on a cliff overlooking Secret Beach. It was longer than I would have liked to have been away, but necessary to support my friend and spend time with our mutual friends. Business was humming along. We had just instituted a new program to build accountability in the construction company, and there was an endless amount of work that needed to be done in all areas of the company. In my shortsightedness, one of the new software programs worked through a smartphone, and I had the only smartphone in the company. On the day of the trip, I traded my phone with my daughter's little brick phone and left my smartphone behind for the company to use for remote data collection. Problem solved. Not quite.

Besides my pack of clothes and adventure gear, I brought along a case full of work that needed finishing before I got back. While my friends were all fired up with getting on a plane to go to Kauai and party, I sat responsibly away from everyone and diligently worked on getting my work done, writing letters on my laptop and making phone calls, working on estimates. I was getting it all done. I continued working on the twenty-minute plane ride, and the ride from the airport to the overnight hotel. I was focused, banging it out, getting shit done! What I didn't realize was everyone else had started their trip and enjoying each other's company. Then life happened.

My daughter's phone did not receive service in any location other than the most metropolitan areas of the island, and our first hotel was already outside of that circle of influence. Then my laptop ran out of power and, wouldn't you know it, in my rush to pack I forgot the charger for the phone and the computer and any writing utensil to continue my work on a yellow pad. I was completely cut off from my work. *Damn!!!*

With nothing left to do but join in the festivities, I joined everyone, grabbed a beer and reconnected with old friends and meet new ones. There was nothing I could do but be present in the situation. It was both my saving grace and my downfall and I wouldn't trade it for the world. I connected with my friends and with myself, finding that my current path did not align with what my heart wanted me to do. I was working myself to an early grave; death of everything except work. It was enlightening to me, and I never heard Jason Mraz's "I'm Yours" more times in my life. Upon my return home, life was different; work was different, I looked at my existing marriage differently; I dressed differently; I spent my time differently.

Shortly after that, I met a friend for coffee. She was having a rough time in her marriage and sounded like she needed a friend to talk to. She vented to me how her marriage had turned for the worse, and she needed some space from it and a friend to spill all her thoughts to. I was glad to provide an ear, but I was not ready for how her feelings would affect me. She poured out how her marriage was not working the way she thought it should. With further digging, I learned that what she wanted out of a marriage wasn't unreasonable, in fact it was pretty modest, but I was living a life that was clearly much less of a marriage than even that. What I was realizing was that her existing relationship was better than the one I was currently in and I shouldn't have been settling for life the way it was. This friend was, of course, Lisa, who became my wife and partner in all things.

The pressure of a bad first marriage blew up several months later when I could not take it anymore and left to sleep on the couch of a friend's house. It was a difficult time, with limited time with the kids, but it gave me space to see clearly what was important to me, what I was willing to accept, and what I could not.

After a week on my own, I returned home with a new purpose to make it work or decide once and for all that it wouldn't. I had a framework to evaluate how things needed to be for me to stay. I had a clear vision of the minimums life had to take for it to be acceptable. In short order, it was clear that my existing marriage would not work and my subsequent moving out and commencement of divorce proceedings happened pretty quickly.

At the tail end of my mid-life crisis, I learned that the marriage I was in was not the direction I wanted. Life was passing me by, and I had not stopped to smell the roses. More importantly, I had spent little time with my kids, who were now teenagers. My mid-life crisis, although painful, put me on my path and gave me clarity on what I needed to live and what I wanted to thrive in life.

The Things We've Learned and the Things We Carry

The true definition of mid-life crisis is a re-evaluation of your life's components and adjustment to your life's direction. Many people have this re-evaluation of their lives, sometimes multiple times, and make changes to their own paths that are usually for the better. That being said, this doesn't mean there is no pain, but there is happiness on the other side of the mid-life crisis.

There are those who think life should have no pain and therefore avoid pain. I, for one, think that is an unfortunate point of view. Life is supposed to be challenging *and joyous*. There are moments of both, and that's how it should be. How would you know times are good without having survived difficulty? The mid-life crisis an opportunity that is painful for a time but can redirect you to where your heart wants you to be.

I know I have more mid-life crises to go through, although since it's unlikely I will attain the ripe old age of 100, it probably shouldn't be called "mid-life." In any case, there will be crises ahead, whether a failed financial position, a health problem or untimely death in the family, or a car accident that has lasting consequences. It may even be the opportunity to move to Puerto Rico, or Europe, or a windfall on a deal that provides other opportunities. While those things do not fall into the category of crisis, per se, they do make you re-evaluate your life, and that's the point. There will inevitably be things that make you re-evaluate your life and what you are doing with the rest of the time you have to spend on earth. These opportunities should be looked at as corrections to make your life uniquely your life; the best of who you are and who you may be.

I know I have plenty of room for improvement and I know these life evaluations make me better each time. The difference this time around is I have a partner I share every thought with who is living through this evaluation of life with me, and our goal is always to improve our relationship. If you have not had a major mid-life crisis in your life, build the relationship with your partner now, so you always have a trusted someone to go through it with you, to talk to about how you are feeling and the unusual thoughts you have. If you are the partner in someone else's mid-life crisis, practice listening intently to understand without judgment and be prepared to ask relative questions to help your partner sort through the confusion. This crisis is something they need help with, but, more often than not, the ultimate decisions are their own, and the support they receive from you is valuable.

If you are in crisis, find out if you can trust your partner with your thoughts and feelings. Test the waters by telling them you are having trouble sorting something out and asking if they can help you by listening without judging. Invite them to ask questions to pull out and explore all the details to help you get more detail or figure out where the holes are for you to either investigate more or figure things out for yourself from there. If that goes well, you have a partner you can trust to go further. For this first conversation, please don't make this first issue about your partner—it would only throw up defenses. This is a test of trust and your ability to be authentic and vulnerable to your partner. Fortunately, this is a quick test, and you will find out several things:

- Whether you can be authentically you and bare your innermost feelings to another person,
- Whether you can verbalize what you feel,
- If your partner is someone you can trust with your feelings, and
- If your partner can actively listen and withhold judgment.

If your answer is yes to all of those things, then you have a good shot at getting through your crisis and making the relationship with your partner even stronger.

Even the Best-Laid Plans...

So life does this thing with the best-laid plans. Often enough, life catches wind of a good plan and throws a fly in the soup, a wrench in the works, changing everything and making you turn directions and start again. This is my story and my past pain. I had a plan, a good one, but my destiny lay elsewhere, and life got in between me and my plan.

My father had a plan, too. He wanted the company he built from the ground up to survive him and be something that would support the family for generations. He was an entrepreneur and leader of leaders. Level-headed, he planned like crazy and worked his butt off. He grew a company that was as stable as a construction company could be, always with state-of-the-art equipment for our locale and what we felt was the strongest company culture around. As he progressed in his growth, he found a leadership role in every endeavor he tried: homeowner's associations, building industry associations, his country club, and especially Rotary. He needed someone to take the reins of the company and keep the ship afloat while he took care of his passions.

Growing up in the business, from sweeping floors to fixing machinery, I had worked in every area of the company, from apprentice to carpenter to foreman to project manager. I had led every department, from operations to purchasing, to setting up the company's accounting system and then moving into sales and estimating. I learned the business from the ground up. I was the heir apparent, knowing my way around every nook and cranny of the company. I had been more involved than any other employee and the only one in my family capable of taking on the role, as I was the oldest by far of my siblings. It was a clean and natural handoff that took nearly twenty years.

Although it had been a long road with bumps and bruises along the way, I had learned a lot about owning and running a business. And while it was still a family company and I kept the advice of my father close, it was my ship to captain. I had grown the company from its twenty to twenty-five employees to a new average of about sixty, with as many as eighty-five employees, and adding a support team to take care of that. We doubled and tripled our gross revenues and spread the wealth among our people. Things were great.

In 2007, there were signs that the economy would tank and I anticipated that action. Our gross sales were dipping, and our margins were getting tighter and tighter. I had seen the signs before with the first and second Gulf wars, and I knew what we should and what we could do. Our little company wasn't so small anymore, and downsizing was painful and challenging. I thought I had the perfect answer, and I was very proud of myself. We evaluated the markets we were in and what markets we thought were impervious to economic downturns, where we could gain expertise and enter to survive the next dip. We changed our marketing efforts to hit specific markets.

We changed our focus to marketing to health care and doctors. People were living longer, and medical technologies were continuing to improve, requiring more facilities to serve people. We looked at marketing to the federal government. Regardless of any economic state, the government always spends money—and lots of it. We also looked at funeral homes. We knew people would continue to die and so it was natural that with more people, there would be more deaths. We felt there would be an expansion of existing mortuaries and new mortuaries popping up. We did great on two of the three markets. Apparently, there were enough funeral homes to go around.

One thing we didn't think of but we benefitted from anyway is that we were already a strong player in the luxury home market. Although there were more competitors in the marketplace, there was also a swell in that market sector, so our workload in that arena continued to be strong.

Health care was excellent; we were working on all the main hospitals on Oahu and building and remodeling doctor's offices and clinics. We were making the right relationships with the facilities managers and getting repeat work logged into our books. We were growing a reputation for high-quality work and proper project management in that arena.

Federal work swelled, but it took some time for us to get our foot in the door. We worked on getting some additional designations to help us find new work. We became a minority-owned business; we moved stock around to my then-wife and became a woman-owned business, and we also attempted (but failed) to get the coveted 8A designation. The hotbed of work in the federal arena was that of military housing, which fit our abilities well.

The downside to that federal work was, although there was a considerable amount of it, privatization was the catchword of the day, and the work was divided into huge chunks that were given to large, international companies. Each of those companies would completely handle their own governance on how they ran the project, regardless of how benevolent or ruthless they might be. They had the work and attracted the players, especially in a tight market. With lots of competition, they could get contractors in for tight margins and hammer people into compliance, but it kept contractors afloat. We were warned about how ruthless some of those large contractors were, but in my arrogance, I was sure I could handle them. We jumped in with both feet.

When other contractors were closing their doors because of the economy, we were in survival mode, but we had more than our fair share of work on the books by changing our markets. 2008 to 2010 were tight for us, but we were surviving and keeping everyone employed and even growing our ranks. Things were going so well in the federal direction that we diminished the amount of work we took in the other areas. Looking back, it was another decision that would soon have impossible consequences.

Then the shit hit the fan. In 2011, we were building a couple of custom homes, remodeling doctor's offices, and making millwork for other general contractors, but primarily we were in the military housing business. The military side kept pushing work our way because we had become one of the most reliable vendors. At the same time, they were getting slower and slower on their payments to us. What I wasn't watching was how quickly our cash flow diminished. We were maxing out our line of credit and were doing what was unadvisable but understandable in survival mode: we were using funds from one job to pay the bills and payroll of the federal projects. By the end of the year, work was flying by; we were hanging on by a thread and stress level was high. Our largest client, who owed us an embarrassing amount of money, refused to help keep things afloat. We were working on the assumption that the client will catch up with payments, but it proved to be wishful thinking.

All the while, the business was in decline, the time spent away and the additional stress on our lives because of the business had taken a grave toll on my already tense marriage. We were at odds already, while trying to keep the kids in the dark about the condition of the company and the marriage. We were wrong in both cases. The kids knew the company was near its demise and the marriage was following suit. Darkness closed in all around me.

Coming off of the holidays, the first quarter of 2012 felt like a little renewal of hope. As we studied the books and looked for alternatives to assist in the survival of the company, it became apparent that we would have to borrow more money if we wanted the company to survive until the next quarter, and the company demise would still be inevitable. Hope was thwarted. For the first time in a long time, things were painfully clear. I decided to close the company and start fresh.

In the weeks before the actual closing, we tediously looked at everything and tried to calculate every move to minimize the damage. Still, there would surely be damage. We wanted to handle things as well as we could, taking care of as many people as we could. We knew it was going to cost a lot of money, but we didn't expect it would be in the millions of dollars to get everything closed. Every review of every account was painful, and there were hundreds of things to look at. Every day I expected to feel like I'd taken a dozen punches to the gut. I knew I had to do it, but it was hard.

We got to the end of the line on March 5, 2012. The weekend had revealed that we wouldn't be able to cover the tax withholding for another week of labor, so we had to stop the labor force from working. March 5 was a Monday, and I called all the superintendents early and had them bring everybody back to the shop for an 8:00 meeting. The mood was somber because people knew the news was not going to be good. While I can remember details of where people were standing and the groups of people who hung around together talking, I can't remember what I was wearing, only that I felt naked and shaken. I knew I had to deliver the news myself. I had laid people off before when we did not have work for people, or we were between projects. Everyone expects that kind of thing in the construction industry. I had never laid off sixty people at once, though. I had my notes put together so that I wouldn't forget any of the points I wanted to say. I waited until I could no longer contain my energy, then, though some people were still missing, I climbed up on one of the table saws in the shop and pulled out my notes. The first few sentences were fine, and then it hit me. This was no longer a plan about closing the company. It was real. We were closing the company, and I fell to pieces. The sobbing seemed to take minutes, although it was probably less than ten seconds; the remainder of my message was shaken but hopefully understandable. It was the hardest thing I have ever done and the longest minutes of my life.

Financially, my parents were ok because throughout the good years they would take money out of the company and sock it away personally, but that did not make them feel good or safe about what was going on. They had only a few things tied to the company that were at risk The biggest was the line of credit that we owed nearly half a million dollars on. I'm so thankful they were able to take on that burden for me, as it allowed me to liquidate everything else in my wealth and the company and clear a big chunk of the slate. Any personal gain I had in my previous marriage I voluntarily relinquished to Pamela as I felt it my obligation to make sure that she landed on her feet. I could not bear to think that the mother of my kids was going to be financially unstable because of the collapse of the company. That was and is an important component for me as a father.

That being said, I know that I was going to start back at zero. In fact, I knew that I would be starting underwater and I had no idea how I was going to dig myself out. There were months of having a giant pit in my stomach that would not go away. I felt like a deer on the road, unable to move because of fear, and the Mack truck was barreling toward me, horn blowing the whole time. There was a constant ringing in my ears, and my nerves kept me shaking regularly. There was no stopping this train until we pulled into our destination. That destination was unknown, but we did know it was going to hurt. We discussed claiming bankruptcy, but in my case, from the claims from a pending lawsuit there would be no protection and the repercussions of the bankruptcy would be hard to overcome. The option was to clear off as many things we were personally liable for and settle with as many people as possible. I met with angry people all the time and needed to be humble and keep my cool. Most people understood, but a few did not, and they had every right to be angry. My decisions had put us in a place that held us back from fulfilling our obligations. Those meetings left me feeling dejected and small, but I knew I had to keep going and meet the next batch of people the following day. Weekends weren't much of weekends, because there was still tons to do, but it was a respite from meeting with people, and I was grateful for the break.

As days turned into weeks and weeks turned into months, the weight on my shoulders got lighter and lighter, or I got stronger and stronger. Sure, there were setbacks when we were thrown a late curve but those diminished over time. Even the strife caused by ongoing litigation eased over time. I still live with the results of the litigation that I feel was wrongly adjudicated, but I have accepted that it is a challenge I will live with and I will get through this as well. I am glad I have an understanding partner in Lisa and good friends who provide me moral support and keep me motivated to move forward.

I had a good solid plan to span the gap of the economic downturn that in the short run worked pretty well, but a couple of specific decisions and the world doing things we did not expect changed the trajectory of my life. At the time, it was a disaster, but looking back at where I was to where I am with Lisa now, I am grateful life changed on me.

Hitting the Bottom

There were a few precursors to hitting the actual bottom, but it makes sense to mention them here. I feel like lots of people who are down on their luck find a similar thing happens to them, where multiple things go wrong at the same time. Whether it be poor planning, snap decisions that were wrong, or just plain bad luck, many people, myself included, spiral out of control toward the ground.

In my case, just before rock bottom, I had gone through my version of a mid-life crisis and had the chance to evaluate the direction of my life and what I wanted more of and less of. The more of was more time of my own with peace and harmony in my life. I wanted a future to look forward to. The less of was pretty much just the opposite, all my waking hours depleted by fighting fires in the company, and a relationship with Pamela that worsened by the day. I no longer wanted to be in the relationship, but I wanted the company to turn the corner with our cash flow problem.

As I massaged the heck out of all the options with the company, unfortunately, I had no control over how to make our largest client to pay on time and problems with the company worsened. So here I was with the marriage going down the tubes, the company continuing to nosedive, and with it, very few of my vendor partners would let up the steam (perhaps thinking I was pulling a fast one). I could tell I was near the bottom when I could not sleep and had little desire to eat. I felt the need to be at the company, but had no moves on the chessboard left to avoid a checkmate.

Fortunately, in my case, there were still fans in my corner, people I highly respected that would tell me that it would take some time, but this would pass, so I was not to let my spirit break. They would tell me stories of people who had failed miserably before they were successful. Stories of Abraham Lincoln, Walt Disney, Thomas Edison, and Vincent Van Gogh were my solace, and close friends like Lisa built me up when my spirit did break. And it did break often, but never permanently. These stories and what they relayed to me were exactly what I needed to internalize to sustain the energy to push through the bottom and claw my way out of the darkness until there was a glimmer of light at the end of the tunnel. That glimmer of light turned out to be a vision of a potential future that was better than the darkness I was in. Once that vision began to brighten, the darkness behind me began to diminish. As I kept pushing forward, the darkness would lose its grip on me.

Now, is that to say that I am entirely out of the darkness? I can't say that; some residual pains follow me around, but they do not have a crippling grip on my being. They are merely small complications that I will have to contend with for some time. Will there be more troubles I will have to fight? You can count on it, but I have the right frame of mind, tools at my side to help me resolve any new issues, and a loving partner who is as committed to me and my success as I am committed to her, her success, and our relationship.

Some say life is 10% what you do and 90% how you react to things that happen to you. Today, I am up for the challenge of making things happen and handling the obstacles thrown into my path. I have a new plan and a new vision that accounts for some wiggle room, and, as a couple, we are committed to heading in that direction until we succeed.

Is this new vision better or worse than the plan I had years ago? Who knows! I do know that I am in a relationship that I *love love love*, I have work I enjoy doing, and I have friends who are close and true. It is a great life I have now and a wonderful future that I want to extend for as long as I can. I also have found an additional purpose that feeds into my primary purpose of being the best husband and partner I can be to Lisa. That new purpose is to help as many people as I can improve their relationships and create a platform that supports those couples who want to take their relationship to its highest potential. We would love for you to be part of that movement.

Epilogue

Don't Stop

Someone asked me yesterday what the most important thing is for improving a relationship. I answered without hesitation: You must have the desire to improve the relationship. You have already shown that you do. All that is required of you now is to decide that you will act, that you'll take the first step toward better relationships, both romantic and otherwise.

Throughout this book, we have outlined different topics important for close relationships. We hope this has prompted questions about your relationships—questions about yourself, questions about your partner (or partner-to-be), questions about the relationship you are in or the one you want to create. If you aren't answering the questions this book has raised for you, reading the book has been a waste. If you do nothing with this knowledge, you will gain nothing from it.

Instead, dig in! Wrestle with your questions! List them, dream about them, journal your innermost thoughts about them. You can decide for yourself what you want and who you want to be. You will gain valuable insight into what you want a relationship to look like and why you want it to be that way.

With this engagement with your questions, you will be armed with the building blocks to create (or recreate) the relationship that this "new you" wants. Okay, I know... It sounds so cut and dry when I say it, but we all know it is not. We are not starting with a clean slate. We all bring into this process our history and experience—our baggage. The work here is hard and sometimes unpleasant. But, if you do the soul-searching to identify yourself and define the life you want to have, the outcome is wonderfully rewarding.

If you have been hurt by a bad relationship, letting your thoughts remain captive, wrapped up in the pain you feel, is the worst place you could be. Learn new strategies to heal yourself, improve your relationships, and thrive!

If you are in a good relationship, my belief is there is always room to improve. I know there is room in my relationship to grow and be a better husband and father. Develop that desire to improve yourself and your relationships and join me on this journey!

At LoveLifeCentral.com, we are developing tools for you, whether you need healing or you just want to grow. We are using our own experiences and collaborating with other experts to come up with strategies we know are effective in creating and maintaining great personal relationships. We are passionate about creating a community to support you in your journey, with workshops and adventure retreats where you can concentrate on improving your relationship.

I hope you feel inspired to continue your journey to better relationships. The world deserves to have change for the positive, especially where relationships are concerned. If we can get enough people to build better relationships with their husbands or wives, perhaps we can have better relations in our communities, better relations within our nations, and better relationships globally. But don't you think that has to start in the home? In *your* home?

This is my passion for the world. I would love for you to reach out and let me know how things are going in your journey, and if there is anything I can do to help you along the way. Strive on, friends!

About the Author

Mike Darcey

Mike Darcey is an entrepreneur who has made a living as a general contractor and construction manager in Hawaii. He is a committed father and husband who's family is an inspiration to him. Mike is a motorcycle fanatic and sings in an acapella barbershop chorus, The Sounds Of Aloha.

The Couple

Mike and Lisa have more than a quarter century of married experience. Unfortunately, they only have 5 years of that experience married to each other. In those 5 years they have gained insightful knowledge on how to best create their loving relationship with each other amidst the trials that life gives us all.